"Gail's story is at once deeply personal and ultimately universal. Her generational insights into love, loss, loyalty— and lots to celebrate — had me turning each page, eager to learn more about the author's story, and myself. A must read!"

— Deborah Grayson Riegel, Keynote speaker and Leadership consultant

"Tender, charming, powerful, *Carrying my Father's Torch* is an exquisite offering to any and all nursing their own legacy wound. We all know of the shadows of our own perception. But what of the shadows cast upon us...even as those shadows may be golden? We become what we know, to be certain. But we can also become the sovereign hero(in)es of our own lives. This glorious read shows us how."

— Tanya Geisler, Leadership Coach

"Gail Gaspar does a beautiful job of weaving family history with personal discovery, in a way that will move anyone wanting to understand how to show up more clearly and powerfully in their own life."

— Pamela Slim, author, *Body of Work* and *Escape from Cubicle Nation*

"For many families, and for certain generations, revealing secrets is fraught with risk. Thankfully, more and more people are learning that it's only in revealing that true healing can take place. Gail Weiss Gaspar reveals, with compassion and guileless truth, a noteworthy father-daughter story. Gail shares how, in encouraging her father to use his voice to tell his story, she is able to claim her own voice and story. Healing intergenerational wounds is one of the greatest gifts an author does for her family. *Carrying My Father's Torch* is a compelling and important example of such a gif

— Karen C.L. Anderson, author
*A Guide fo

D1167175

"Unpacking the earned wisdom gleaned from her profession as a coach and from her childhood experiences, Gail Gaspar offers stories and direction for how to overcome inherited trauma and liberate the Divine spark within each of us. Compelling, raw and illuminating, this book will give you the courage to explore your own life's experiences and the legacies you have inherited, and let these guide you."

— Hiro Boga, Award-winning author, Business strategist, Mentor

"Taking on the complex and the taboo, Gail Gaspar unravels her life with uncommon directness, clarity, and simplicity. Unvarnished, she immediately connects with the reader and never lets go. Gaspar unpacks and carefully puts pain, shame, even confusion in its place. Gaspar is a gifted writer with something very important to say."

— Amy Kaslow, Writer and photographer, covers at-risk societies worldwide; Presidential appointee to the United States Holocaust Memorial Museum

"Can a child of Holocaust survivors tell about her life without being overshadowed by her parents' legacy of suffering? With an authentic voice, Gail Weiss Gaspar weaves memories of her own childhood into the evolving adult relationship with her survivor father and a mother pained by her own tragedies. In her moving account, various strands of the past and present are stitched together to form a patchwork of memories until a carefully crafted quilt emerges...a beautiful tapestry that gives touching testimony to a daughter's adult journey with her father. It is only after her father becomes a public speaker that the family's code of silence about his survival in Auschwitz and Mauthausen is broken. With Gail's book, we have received the gift of a soul-searching memoir of the second-generation. As Marty's daughter, Gail movingly describes her childhood recollections of growing up in a house of silences and how she, as an adult, lovingly reconnected to her father as he began to speak publicly about his survival."

— Björn Krondorfer, Director of The Martin-Springer Institute and Professor of Religious Studies, Northern Arizona University

CARRYING
MY
FATHER'S
TORCH

CARRYING MY FATHER'S TORCH

From Holocaust Trauma to Transformation

GAIL WEISS GASPAR

Oceanwalk Press

Published by Oceanwalk Press

Editors: Deborah Kevin and Joyce Moss
Cover and Interior Design: Christy Collins
Publishing consultant: Martha Bullen
Illustration of Author: Michael Gaspar
Author Photo: Michael Kress

ISBN (Paperback): 978-1-7358142-0-9
ISBN (ebook): 978-1-7358142-1-6

Printed in the United States of America

For Maurice, whose unconditional love makes me brave.

For our children, Michael and Stephanie,
who light up my life.

For my parents, Marty and Joan.

Foreword

"Who would want to hear my story?" asks Marty Weiss.

This book tells Marty's personal life story, his experiences and the events of his life. But it is much more besides. It is the story of the persecution and suffering of an entire family. A story of those people who did not survive, of those who did survive and have to live with that, but also of those generations who came later, who cannot get away from it, even many years later.

What is more, it is part of the story of humanity as a whole. The story of the loss of humanity. The story of hate, fear, violence and inhuman suffering. The story of looking away and acquiescence.

It is also the story of finding humanity again. The story of being with each other and for each other, the story of rising up and being strong. The story of survival, of living.

Marty's life story is therefore our story too. We were and are a part of it. This is what we must learn from it, and this is what we must never forget.

Dear Marty. Thank you for being such an inspiration to us all, again and again. Dear Gail, thank you for carrying forward the memory of your family with this book.

Celebrate life, every day anew.

In wholehearted solidarity,

Barbara Glueck
Director of the Mauthausen Memorial
Mauthausen, Austria

PROLOGUE

If you have ever said to yourself, "How could I possibly break free from my family's past? I am not enough, and it's too late to be the person I hoped I'd be," this book is for you. If you muzzled your true nature with critical self-talk—relentless nay-saying that insists, convincingly, on hurling statements like, "I am alone. I don't know how. I can't. I'm not ready. I don't know what's next," this book is for you.

I am the child of two deeply wounded parents, a parent myself, and a professional career and life coach. Over the years, I've struggled to separate my fate from theirs, their agonizing past from my present. How do I reconcile with my family's and my legacy? A Holocaust survivor father and a mother abandoned by her parents, two victims of their own traumas.

It happened this way. For years, I went along with all that was asked of me. When the decades of compliance made me ill, I became the one who asked why. This once obedient girl discovered there was more to lose than reputation or others' judgment by accepting what they expected of me.

I always thought my story was less important in light of my father's story. He was a hero. Then, the truth unraveled like a skein of yarn, revealing that my story, while interwoven with his, is truly my own, is worth telling. It's easier to project heroism onto another instead of claiming it for ourselves.

What if, instead of looking backward or outward to life's easily identifiable heroes, we looked inside ourselves? What if our evolution can lead to triumph—despite, and partially due to our family wound or cultural history? What if the human spirit can soar above what once seemed impossible to accomplish in that context? Regardless of who and what came before us, what would it be like for you and me to see ourselves as the heroes of our own story?

Yes, this book is partly about one's man's strength, about what it took to survive, about the extraordinary ordinariness of much, though not all, of his life, and what it can teach us about living ours with greater urgency and meaning. But it's also about how growing up steeped in that environment kept me from recognizing that a hero dwelled inside me, too.

Are you a child who absorbed trauma from your family legacy or from other relationships?

What do we owe those who came before us? I have come to believe we ought to carry their legacy and add ingredients of what is raw, authentic, and evolving in ourselves—to identify and take a stand for what we believe—in our work and life.

I've crafted a story of meaning from a legacy of suffering. If I've done it well, you'll read it as a story of transformation—from sorrow and shame to joy and courage. You'll appreciate that transformation is a journey requiring exploration and an intention to mine for meaning. You'll use it for clues to uncover for yourself how to overcome resistance and legacy limitations as you consider your (un)conscious legacy conditioning.

By the time you finish reading this book, my hope is you will feel compelled to face your *legacy wound* and use it to create a meaningful life for yourself and others, at any age or stage. That you, too, will learn to repurpose the pain to update your story in a way that allows you to become a more authentic, confident, and sovereign version of yourself.

1

An interesting thing about heirlooms, though sadly I had none in the traditional sense, was that I inherited qualities instead of tchotchkes.

What if heirlooms are not only ornaments and sepia photographs, but also *legacy attributes*, waiting to be unpacked? Imagine if what's in the steamer trunk is a thorn, coaxing a persistent, yet reluctant, dream?

2

My father, Martin Weiss—Marty to most—discovered his voice when he was in his sixties. His visible identity was that of *husband, father, and butcher,* with his full story, selectively sealed off from family and himself. He would say walling off those memories was necessary to move beyond his unspeakable pain and loss. As a 15-year-old, he lost a mother, a father, three sisters, a brother, and suffered his own horrific internment, hunger, and hard labor.

Growing up, I never remember him complaining or saying he wished things were different though he must have felt this way every day. Dad never spoke about the traumas he experienced during World War II. Moving on *from them* was the only way he saw to have a chance at living a normal life. In his way, he was protecting us, and others, from the atrocities he'd experienced. His ultimate kindness? Not ever insinuating that the pain in our lives was in any way diminished or incomparable to his.

The biggest regret of Dad's life was that he did not receive a formal education beyond the eighth grade because of the war. Yet the moment he stepped up to the podium at age sixty-three to tell his story at the United States Holocaust Memorial Museum (USHMM), he became someone who educated others. He did not decide to do so easily.

When my parents moved to Washington, D.C. from New Jersey to be closer to my growing family, I reached out to the Holocaust Survivor liaison at the USHMM, leaving message after message. The staffer didn't return my calls, and it felt impossible to pin him down about bringing Marty in for an initial conversation.

On the home front, Marty was unsure about getting involved with the Museum. Frequently he said, "Who would want to visit a museum about the Holocaust?" and "No one wants to hear my story." Finally, Marty mustered up the courage to say, "Yes, I'll do it." He doubted there was a place for him there. Proof positive was that, despite my overtures to the museum, they had not contacted him. We went back and forth for months.

I knew he was afraid to be visible, vocal in a way he had never been. For years, he'd toiled as a butcher in a blood-stained white apron. Never before had he organized thought, memory, and meaning for an audience. Never before had he stood onstage and spoken in his English-tinged-with-Czech accent through a microphone. His mettle and story were untold, untested. He went about his life, keeping it to himself, *sparing others* who could not understand. Where stories of the Holocaust were shared across platforms and thousands of times by others, he had a lifetime of silence under his belt. Oh, his unique and compelling story burned inside him, but the pilot light was out.

When the day came for Marty's first presentation, my mother, Joan, and I sat on cushioned seats in the front row of the cavernous auditorium. My heart pounded, and my entire body felt frozen, uneasy. I dared not turn around to survey the auditorium. Dad speaking his story out loud is what I had envisioned for years. *How would he handle being the center of attention? What if he stuttered, or forgot what he wanted to say? What if he broke down in tears? What if he froze? Or failed?*

Seeing him on stage, gripping the podium as if to steady himself, my breathing grew shallow, my fingers fidgety. I kept my eyes glued to his face for the first sign of distress or regret, as though by my very will, I could protect him. Right before he spoke his first words, I allowed a slight turn of my head to look around. The air hummed with conversation as hundreds of strangers—students, teachers, and parents—filled the seats, some even standing in the aisle. They were all curious to hear my father's story.

Mom turned to me and said, "Doesn't your dad look handsome? Finally, he is dressed in a suit and tie."

In hindsight, the occasion of bearing witness to the telling of his story out loud was pivotal, not only for Dad and Mom but also for me, a step in however many degrees of separation it would take me to claim my own.

3

It is hard to exaggerate the role *The Store* played in our lives. We always called it that, *The Store*, a tangible character in our family story, which just happened to be built of brick and mortar. We never called it *his* store, *our* store, or even its actual name. This much I knew. The Store was master of us, not the other way around. The Store was the cause of Dad's heart condition, financial worries, and a perpetual state of exhaustion. The Store was the reason we rarely went on family vacations. The ever-present reason we subsisted.

Marty became what he knew: His father had been a farmer and butcher; his mother, a nourisher of her children's stomachs and dreams. At age sixteen, he arrived in America, minus parents, half his siblings, his friends, and an education. Being a butcher allowed him to be his own boss, maintain his independence. Yes, the decision to work as a butcher fed our family, but it came at a tremendous cost.

Sometimes our instincts do not serve us. His instinct was to work hard, to work for work's sake, to the point of exhaustion, and then repeat. It evolved into a pattern of life that became his identity. As long as he owned The Store, the pattern would never let up, would never show signs of compromise or change.

The Store was Marty's chance at a good-enough life, independence from older siblings, and was a major consideration in every decision my parents made. It was the bane of my mother's existence. The Store competed for her attention, enflamed marital arguments, and usually won out over what she wanted.

As a *character* in our family story, The Store had its own physicality. There was a shopping section for customers. Polished chrome cases framed slanted glass, a window to meat and seafood cases on one side, cold cuts on the other. Scales on top of showcases to weigh merchandise, containers to weigh slaw and macaroni salad. Groceries on the other side, neatly stacked on shelves, labels always facing out. Boxes and crates of merchandise yet to be stocked—soda, canned goods. A display or two at the front for point of purchase items like Lay's potato chips and Drakes' yodel cakes. Handwritten signs, in large letters on oak tag, advertised specialties like crown roast and lobster tails. Posters of meats, cheeses, and hindquarters taped to the walls up to the ceiling. Large black and white tiles spanned the floor where, when The Store was quiet, as a child, I'd play hopscotch.

Then, there were the spaces customers could not see. The backroom had a sign, splattered, tacked and tilted on the door: *Keep Door Closed, Employees Only.* The backroom is where the magic happened. When I think of The Store, I recall it through the senses of taste and smell. Every couple of days, Dad cooked up highly seasoned roast beef, turkey, and ready-made meals to go in a once-white oven that looked like a relic from the First World War. Some customers timed their shopping with his cooking. They'd appear when a highly seasoned roast beef or turkey came out of the oven. The aroma of garlic and pepper delighted the nose, intensifying when the cooking was nearly done.

Still, I'd ask, "When will it be ready?" as my stomach rumbled, eager for that first slice hot out of the oven. I typically turned down the end piece, so Dad ate that. He knew I liked roast beef best right out of the oven, rare and sliced ribbon-thin. Each time, though he knew I'd never say, "No," he'd ask if I'd like some. Then he'd hand me a slice with a bright pink center.

Another place mostly out of sight to customers was behind the long meat counter. It was lined with weathered butcher blocks and sharp tools of the trade: diamond knives, cleavers, a slicing machine. I remember the day Dad invested in a new slicer; it was as if he'd bought a Cadillac. Taking it for a spin, he demonstrated its fine features: sensitive adjustments for slicing thickness, greater speed, the gentle glide required to move the slicer back and forth.

I had to wait until I was older before he'd let me use it. I was eager to move behind the counter and take this task off his shoulders. When I could, it made me feel like I was part of a team. The machine whirred as my hand moved the cheese or pastrami back and forth over the blade to get slices the weight and thickness each customer asked for.

I would play a game with myself to guess the correct weight right before placing deli items on the scale. If it was something I liked, I'd put a slice or two aside on a thin piece of wax paper to eat later, when the butchers slugged down black coffee. To my disappointment, I wasn't tall enough to reach over the counter to offer samples, as my father liked to do. Although I still made change "on the other side, the clean side" of the counter space (my mother's reference), I came to prefer my Keds in sawdust, fingers seasoned with cold cuts.

Was it here I first learned core values I would carry forward? The value of hard work. The curiosity and learning that comes from social interaction. The importance of integrity. The sense of worth that comes from getting paid for work well done. Was it here I learned to distinguish my preferences from my mother's?

4

"Don't argue in front of the children," Joan would often say in the evenings after Marty returned home, weary from a hard day's work. Then they'd head off to their bedroom, shut the door, and continue arguing in a less audible manner. They usually fought about money (how she spent it) or expectations (why she wouldn't work in The Store). Also, Joan didn't like rules—she felt they need not apply to her—whereas Marty was a rule follower. Hearing their disagreements unnerved me. When plugging forefingers in my ears didn't work, I'd go to my room and turn up my music. Their expressions of anger scared me.

On the one hand, I was always taught to keep a polite, civilized tone. On the other, their arguments took place behind a slammed closed door. My anger felt off-limits, and I was still years away from allowing myself the fuller expression of acknowledging it.

Mom was as childlike as she was charming. Her favorite meals out were hamburgers and fries at McDonald's or pizza, and we'd go often. When she packed my lunchbox, friends envied the array of junk food that accompanied my white Wonder bread sandwiches. Her wishes were straightforward—and unrelenting. When she decided she wanted to go out for pizza, or that it was time to go on a vacation, or that I cut my flowers stems too short, she wouldn't let go until there was acquiescence or an argument. Mom's favorite outing was shopping with me. A few times a year, she would take me to the fancy mall about thirty minutes from home. "We're just here to window shop," she said when the sales lady approached. We'd get there just as The Store opened. We'd *oooh* and *aaah* at pretty clothing, finger the elegant fabrics, then leave for lunch, empty-handed.

Even though Joan didn't buy at fancy stores, she always looked well put together. She made outward appearance a priority. Joan never left home without makeup or hair done. Her eyes were blue as cornflowers, skin soft as peaches. Mostly, her brunette hair was dyed double-process blond. Where I grew up, it was not uncommon for some mothers to wear curlers in their hair in public. "There's no excuse for that," she said. "A husband likes it when his wife cares about her appearance." Joan held true to her interpretation of the feminine role and values—of this, she was proud and unapologetic. Marty held true to his interpretation of hard work and the value of human life. More fodder as I mined for how to construct my views on feminine and human values.

5

*P*erfection is a preoccupation perfectly suited to spinning *a perception* of safety in one's life. In truth, the pursuit of perfection is a goalpost that shifts like grains of sand on a windy day. As a result of the years of being praised for pleasing others, my good grades, judgement, and mature disposition around adults, I thought the goals I held most dear would always be just beyond reach. Was I striving for perfection out of guilt? The supreme privilege of being born free in America was something deeply rooted in my understanding, as was the supreme privilege of being born. Striving for perfection seemed the least I could do.

6

"We are private people. Don't trust anyone but family," my mother repeatedly said throughout my childhood. My family had secrets, as all families do. It became my job to be our family's secret keeper. For that, I needed an outlet—a safe one. My journal was that harbor.

I've written in journals since I was seven. The consistency pleased me. The habit gave me a window into my soul, and a record of my days, even when it was used only to complain about gloomy March rain or make a note of the savory lamb chops I ate. *But in journaling, there was no volume button, zero chance of being heard.* As long as I wrote and kept my thoughts private, my story and my family were *safe.*

From the unfulfilled desire to write my own story came a core recognition: years cloaked in loyalty to *the code of silence.* Dad never spoke of his wartime experience to my brother or me. Didn't speak of it to Mom, who didn't ask him about it. Neighbors and friends dismissed what had happened as *something that occurred over there, in Europe.* For reasons he still can't explain, he and his surviving siblings never discussed the concentration camps at all. Was the experience too horrific for words? The inner pain too fierce? The drive to leave it behind too unrelenting?

I grew up only knowing what I could glean of Marty's story. His story, not mine. I grappled with questions. Was his story mine to tell? How could I do it justice? Say it right? My father, who, as a child of fifteen, survived when half his family, his village did not. I owed him. Owed them all.

But what did I owe? Unbroken silence? Keeping myself buried in the pages of my journals as I have since childhood? Whom was I protecting? What was I refusing to own? How did I melt my resistance to telling my story, my experience of being down, then getting up and moving through it? Knowing before I knew, that a life exposed could be seized upon and extinguished without warning.

Like many first-generation children of trauma survivors, I grew up thinking I knew Dad's story as if it were encoded in my DNA. As his first-born daughter, I needed to exist as the opposite of the darkness he endured; I needed to demonstrate being worthy of life itself.

I found myself in the crossroads of permission. The possible bearer of truth, in hopes that it would help others to permit themselves to amplify their gifts, to be who they must be rather than die with their story still inside.

Over shared hot pastrami on rye in our favorite diner, I decided to speak to Marty about writing our story, seeking his blessing. I needed to come to terms with my fear in terms of the invitation, not the forbidden territory. The blistered vinyl of the booth seat stuck to my thighs, creating a crisscross pattern that, when I stood, would be visible beneath my blue shorts.

I took a deep breath to meet his unsuspecting gaze. "I'm writing a memoir. About you. Mom. The Store. Me."

He gazed intently and leaned toward me over the faux marble table. "You know," he said, "at one time, I thought I would write a book about my experience. I wish I had a way with words. But you were always *the Writer* in the family."

And there it was, the generosity and kindness, positivity and love that Marty held in his heart, despite the devastating inhuman experiences he had faced, situations designed to annihilate both body and soul. He gave me his blessing to give voice to our story. I was ready to risk it.

7

In college psychology 101, a homework assignment was to chart our family tree. Mine had two branches: my parents and their parents. I watched in wonder as classmates presented their family line, fanned out across pages. Some even boasted a family crest or motto. In my case, it was *loss re-imagined* in a new and visible form.

I have one heirloom—Aunt Ellen's silver roasting pan. Pitted on the inside, a handle on each side, it's too unwieldy to hang on a wall or display on a shelf, yet it is worthy of the position. On visiting Sundays, I sat on her speckled Formica counter as she cooked meals from the old country. From memory, never a recipe. Her mouthwatering sweet and sour stuffed cabbage is the meal I remember most. Its ingredients and preparation were secret. It took many years for her to agree to teach my mother how to make it.

I imagine Aunt Ellen standing over the pot, stirring, in a stained cotton blouse, its long sleeves rolled to the elbows. Ellen was the oldest daughter in a family wracked by loss. On Sunday, her only day off from their store, she created what it tasted like to be home before the war—sweet scent of paprika—the smell of home when all else that defined home was gone.

My dad is the sole receptacle of collective family memory. He is the last person of his family still standing. It strikes me—*what he does not remember, we will never, never know.*

8

Discipline. A powerful word, a rigorous practice. Perhaps it is what saved Dad. When he is asked, "Why did you survive when others didn't?" he does not use the word discipline. But at fourteen, he developed the instinct, a self-imposed discipline that may very well have saved him. Perhaps this explains his pragmatism, his utter absence of drama or doubt that he would step up and do what needed to be done. Without self-pity or complaint.

Dad's work ethic, to me, seemed inhuman. He went to The Store six or seven days a week, worked ten to fourteen hours a day. We took one week of family vacation a year. He had strong values, particularly of dependability. If customers wanted to shop, he would be there to serve them.

Once there was a big nor'easter snowstorm that made driving impossible. When Dad couldn't get his car out of the driveway, he trudged three miles over unplowed roads and through high snow banks. All so that he could turn the key in the lock and open The Store. The other workers didn't show up. Maybe there were a handful of customers. After dark, he walked back home. The walk alone took him hours. We thought he was nuts and told him so. But we could not stop him from opening The Store. What if a customer came and he was not there? He would not disappoint his customers.

Discipline, independence, and reliability were values that became internalized, rooted in me too. What I observed was Dad's absolute adherence, many times exacted at a high cost to himself. As an adult and as a mother, by default, I did much the same. I put others' needs and wants before my own. I did not realize then that the level of allegiance to those values was something I got to choose.

9

In our household, laziness was a non-starter, simply not tolerated.

"Time to get up!" Dad's early morning command rang into our sleepy ears before he left for work, even on weekends.

Being *unproductive* was the worst offense. Time was meant for work. Productivity was an expectation that surrounded us at all times. I either was or was not productive. Mostly, I found that I wasn't, that I didn't live up to high levels of output. But each day, I'd get up and try again. I swallowed, hook, line, and sinker, the expectation to be productive, and interpreted being productive enough as a cue to be taken from others. Expectations were high, the needle for it kept moving, and I kept coming up short.

I absorbed Dad's belief that every moment must be productive and engaged with the types of learning that eluded him at a young age. Productivity created a tense relationship with time and with my perception of "wasting time," before I separated myself enough to reconsider the concept. Among other issues, the years I spent childrearing, when most women were working, were often fraught with inner conflict. The gift of being able to be present with our children versus the guilt of not helping the world by developing me in a broader sense...the in-between, the not knowing how or if I would ever step off the mommy platform, was at times as debilitating as it was a remarkable privilege.

I took his example to heart and performed work with a known outcome, which meant "was I likely to succeed?" My father made enough money to support basic needs for our family and maintained his freedom from working "for somebody else." The work itself was hard, a struggle. All these years, I've considered writing a luxury I could not afford when measured in time and attention. It seemed frivolous, not work measured in sweat and struggle, not productive as I understood the meaning of the term.

There was a moment, writing this, when I audibly gasped, realizing there was a metal sign hanging above the entrance to Auschwitz, which said, *Arbeit Macht Frei.* "Work makes you free." The sign was erected by prisoners with metalwork skills on Nazi orders in June 1940. My gut seized up. In this way, and never intending to, I would be letting "them" win if I continued to work just for work's sake. If I kept silent about what I knew.

10

The journals I kept as a young girl were everything to me. A gold padlock sealed secrets between flowery covers. A dainty key let me believe my words were safe. In each new diary, I wrote on each first page in big, bold letters: PRIVATE. DO NOT READ. To this day, I do not know if anyone defied my decree. I needed a place to say what I knew inside but could not express to my parents, who would not understand, or my friends, whom I might not be able to trust.

I was not conscious that I was actually hiding and did not wish to be found. I did not intend to keep myself from becoming who I needed to be. The parental models I had taught me to value safety first. It stemmed from their learned experience–and that kept me silent for years. After all, their most significant wounds came from risking "exposure."

This much I knew: Thoughts insisted on becoming words on paper. They filled notebooks, napkins, ripped remnants of paper, which were stored in deep, covered boxes in the basement. Never read. Only stored in the dark.

What no one tells you: how your insides suffer when inimitable expression stays buried deep inside you, dark and captive to fear. For a would-be painter, the expression might be a portrait or landscape painting with their unique flourish on it; for a would-be chef, a tantalizing dish with an original blend of ingredients; for a would-be improv performance artist, a way to make personal wounds and what others take for granted visible.

Dad struggled to come up with what to write about for his Holocaust writing class. He praises what others manage to put to paper, but *his own stories*, he tells me, *fall short*. He sends me a story to spell-check. A story I've not heard before, written in detail as crisp as though it happened yesterday. And it moves me. Moments like this, his unfurling of memory, and I can't tell what shapes me more–*what I know* or *what he's left unsaid*.

11

*A*ttachments. I have long wondered about the sacred bond Dad, and I share. The unspoken depth of mutual understanding, respect, and sensibility. Pictures of steer that papered walls up to the ceiling at *The Store*. In particular, the arrow to connective tissue, called fascia, that was invisible to the eye. It was beneath the animal skin. Fascia attaches, stabilizes, and separates muscles and other internal organs. In yoga class, stretching the fascia is like clearing out cobwebs between the muscles, allowing them to glide more efficiently to increase hydration and eliminate toxins. It is as if Dad and I are connected beyond the mind. As if we are mysteriously, invisibly, connected by fascia.

12

As a young girl, I saw how neighbors and customers pigeonholed my dad. *Martythebutcher.*

"What does your father do?" my friends' parents would ask.

Unwilling to admit it, I would say, "He owns a store," or "He provides meat to institutional cafeterias." Yes, these things were true. Also true: there was a time I would dress up the word, *butcher,* due to my shame, my private sorrow.

Unlike his older brother, who owned a kosher butcher shop like their father in the old country, Marty opened a store that sold ham, sausages, kielbasa, and shellfish. Ever the pragmatist, he recognized that there was a broader market for non-kosher food. After what he'd experienced in the war, he rejected the orthodox practices of his childhood. For a time, he lost faith in religion, *but he never lost his faith in people.* He consistently demonstrated the belief that most people are inherently good.

When I turned eight, Marty said to me, "You're old enough to help out on the register."

I felt pleased that he trusted me. He taught me how to give change, practicing at home using the bills and coins in his weathered black wallet. Once he felt confident in my counting abilities, we went on a Sunday when The Store was closed and practiced on the shiny chrome cash register that sat tall on the counter.

Because I was small for my age, I stood on a stool to reach the black and white dime-size register keys, which required some muscle to press. It was slow going at first to find the right keys to match the price sticker on each can of creamed corn or half-pound of country ham. The best part of working the register was the BING of the *total* key, proclaiming for all within earshot that a sale was complete and signaling for the cash drawer to spring open.

"Look the customer in the eye, and say, "Thank you," Dad taught me. "Always keep the bill out, never push the drawer in until you count the change back, out loud, to the customer."

I started work on a Saturday because it was the busiest day in The Store. The scruffy assistant butchers were not allowed to touch the register—only Dad and me. I saw myself as an integral part of The Store, as the last point of contact before customers scooped their paper bags, carried their groceries out the door, and went about their day.

Although my brother, Jeff, also started working in The Store by eight years old, his experience was different than mine. On Saturday mornings, he'd watch his friends meet at the bottom of our street as he waved from the passenger seat on the way to work. His first job was as dishwasher of large pots and pans in the Employees Only backroom. He stood on a red plastic milk crate to perform the assigned task. Also, barely able to see over the workspace, he bagged deli paper wrapped items left by the men on the butcher blocks. He swept sawdust, Windexed the cases, and did whatever chores needed to be done. When Jeff reached his teens, he and Dad bucked heads on anything from how to package salami to how to keep The Store up-to-date. Their points of view rarely converged, provoking a conflict that went on between them for years.

My dad often yelled at Jeff for perceived wrongs. Jeff was left feeling he couldn't do anything right. To refuse to work in The Store would have been to deny him. My brother and I wouldn't have dreamed of doing so. Somehow, we sensed he had suffered enough.

The silver lining of working in The Store, for Jeff, was that Dad's relentless determination and work ethic rubbed off. It infused in him a "no excuse for inaction" mentality and instilled in him a reactive insistence on creating a life that consisted of work *and* play. Key takeaways were similar to mine that there needed to be more life balance, time for leisure; that putting in effort and taking responsibility were required, not optional.

13

As a child, I watched for Mom's moods as one sits perched and alert for oncoming storm clouds. When her blue eyes turned cloudy and cool, the corners of her mouth drooped, and her rouged cheeks paled, she'd crumble. Powerless, she'd retreat to her room, the door pulled, shades drawn.

In my teens, my mother was diagnosed with manic depression, which is now called bipolar disorder. The doctor told her it likely was brought on by the maternal rejection she'd experienced at seventeen, when she and her two sisters were asked to move out of their home.

Their mother had been a young widow. When she remarried, her new husband made it clear he did not want any children in the house. Her mother remained silent and watched, as one by one, her three daughters were cast adrift.

A sense of abandonment pierced Mom's sense of self like shards of glass. With nowhere to go, she bounced from relative to relative with no sense of home or belonging. She struggled the rest of her life from pain caused by her mother's wholesale disinterest, passivity, and rejection.

Her level of functioning could plummet by the day or season. Or due to an encounter with her mother or argument with my father. Mom would not recover, without incident, from her feelings of abandonment. As a child, I knew in my bones when it was time for me to step up my responsibilities around the house. Without any exchange between us, I knew to keep quiet, not tell a soul. I never knew when a breakdown would end. One day, the cloud (as she called it) would lift, and she was our mother again.

Despite her challenges, Mom, guided by Dad, was determined to parent her children differently, and better, than how she was raised. She stayed at home to be with my brother and me. Committed to infusing us with a sense of belonging and confidence that she never had.

When I was a teenager, I chided her for not working outside the home. How my barbed words must have hurt. I didn't realize that, given her dramatic mood shifts, combined with a lack of education and training, she may not have been able to hold down a job. The idea that Mom should strive to be an independent woman in her own right in the time of women's lib was a stance I would not relinquish. My attitude caused a chasm between us. Because she could not give me all I needed, I rejected her life choices until I became a parent myself.

Wouldn't it be wonderful if we were rich? Mom often fanaticized aloud about circumstances that lay beyond our reality. Above all, stories that amplified love had her smitten—silver screen love, like *Gone with the Wind*, *Beauty and the Beast,* and *Dr. Zhivago.* She'd watch certain movies again and again. Mom's world may have been small, yet she dared to dream. At the core of her parenting, my brother and I understood that she wanted us to dream, too.

As a child, Joan took piano lessons. Dad bought an upright, dark walnut Wurlitzer so she could play—and so my brother and I could take lessons. When Mom was mad or sad, she'd sit down at the piano. Over and over again, her fingers pounded feverishly across the familiar keys, evoking unmistakable suffering. Although the trauma was different than my father's, her wound went to the marrow and filled all the space in our house. It reached us at a cellular level, as she played the same sad song, the one song she'd committed to memory: the Warsaw Concerto. Eerily, it conjured both their pasts.

14

The most secret place in The Store, pitch black except for a few bare bulbs from the ceiling and insulated by vault-thick doors, was one I mostly avoided: The meat freezer, where pervasive fatty odors got into the nose and lingered. It is where hinds of beef were delivered through the alley door in the dark morning hours directly from New York City's meatpacking district. Dad prided himself on only selling the finest quality meat. Sometimes eight or more hindquarters hung from the ceiling on protruding silver hooks.

As a child, I was afraid of being locked inside the meat freezer, surrounded by carcasses in temperatures that made me shiver. Not so the couple of butchers hired to assist Dad with the cold and backbreaking task of taking down and carving the hindquarters. Fortified by to-go cups of black diner coffee, men in aprons disappeared into the freezer all day long with one purpose, to deconstruct what was hanging and package it into portions for customers.

Although Dad insisted the whole family needed to help, my mother never worked even one day in The Store. She refused. On days she couldn't wait for items she needed to make dinner, she'd walk through the door of The Store, the jingle of the bell overhead announcing her arrival.

Joan despised The Store and the role of butcher's wife that defined her. "It's the reason why," she said, "I never really belonged to the sisterhood of women whose husbands wore knotted ties, carried briefcases, and commuted to the city by train."

I did not have a word for it then, but in retrospect, I sense what she felt was "shame." Had I inherited some of my shame from her? Or was it all mine? How much did this part of my identity influence me?

The wives of Marty's brother and brother-in-law both worked in their husbands' butcher stores, putting in long hours, toiling at the register, and serving customers. Marty expected nothing less. Still, Joan stayed away. It seemed to me she never stood her ground more firmly, acted more emboldened, than in her refusal to put in even one hour of work there. Marty viewed her defiant stance as wholly disloyal. Perhaps she saw The Store as competition for his time and attention. She was certain it was no place for a woman to be among meat and sawdust. Their disparate viewpoints caused many arguments behind closed doors.

I can still hear the prickle in my mother's words.

"I wish it weren't this way," she'd say, followed by, "Marty, why can't you wear a suit and tie to work?"

15

My mother signed up to chaperone on my class trips and as a Girl Scout troop leader. She was not always up for it, but she tried to go anyway. She did not take for granted that my father *allowed* her to stay home with us (her mother, when single with three young daughters, was forced to work when all her friends' mothers were home for their children). Yet staying home often bred a sense of isolation and depression in her (as in many other of the nearly sixty percent of stay-at-home moms in the U.S. in the 1960s). She'd serve our favorite foods—like macaroni and Velveeta cheese—when we came home for lunch and on weekends. Put out Oreo cookies and milk for our friends and us after school.

At the time, I had no idea she was making it up as she went. Her father died when she was seven. Her mother proved incapable of showing love. She had no example of what a loving mother did. Yet, in this sense, she was determined. She was making up for parental shortcomings in her own childhood, changing the story her single mother had spun, demonstrating love to dad, my brother, and me, knowing it could be lost—all without charting a fulfilling enough course for herself—so far.

In our neighborhood, it was not uncommon to hear through open windows husbands lording it over their wives, and we saw more than one chase his wife or son across the lawn with a belt. Some mothers found escape in alcohol or valium. Kept messy homes. We had neighbors and friends who imagined we lived a perfect life.

Although Mom did not work outside the home, she was creative and loving. Helping us with school projects, at various times painting (by numbers—a landscape of hers hung framed in the hall), and, later, sculpting. She crafted a maypole for my six-year-old birthday and found ways to make holidays and gatherings feel special. She volunteered at a hospice for over a decade and came home with stories of how fulfilling it was to read to patients. She'd apply lotion to chapped hands, paint their fingernails with her signature platinum polish, and hang construction paper signs in the room, signs on which she crayoned, "You're special."

I often asked her, "Isn't it depressing? You know the patients are going to die. Yet you get close to them."

She did not find it depressing in the least—she took pleasure in most patients assigned to her and felt sad when they died. She also loved that they loved her.

Despite her lack of education beyond high school and lack of worldly exposure, Mom was street smart and resourceful. She collected S&H green stamps and traded them in for appliances. Knew how to strike a bargain. She placed classified ads in the local newspaper. Strangers would respond to her advertisements, coming to our backyard or basement to retrieve their purchases. I watched in amazement as she, more times than not, convinced them that they needed what she was selling. I have clear recollections of men hauling away old RCA TVs, women carrying off her worn wigs (!), and old hairdryers…things that Mom no longer had any use for. They'd pay her in cash.

Other mom-isms were not so helpful to me. Joan taught me things like women are jealous and judgy (how early I absorbed that girls could not be trusted). The way to be loyal to the family is to make sure everything that happens in the family stays private (how quickly I became adept at keeping secrets). A woman's role is to make her man happy (how well I learned that making a man happy was more important than my happiness).

Though I didn't always agree with her, some of her views seeped into my subconsciousness. It took decades to discern where they kneecapped my aspirations for self-expression, connection, and fulfillment.

My mother instructed me not to expect anything from people, that they would disappoint me, resulting in me getting hurt. That this was her experience was undeniable. She carried scars from expecting her mother to be a mother to her. Of relying on others to take her in and nurture her. She tried to protect us from feeling that way. And I dutifully carried her truth as my own.

I was a girl in search of strong, independent female role models. But Jeff, my younger brother, remembered aspects of our mother that I either didn't see or had forgotten: unconditional love for us reflected in her pale blue eyes and dash of silly that tempered Dad's serious nature. Mom defended Jeff to our father when he performed poorly in school.

We shared the same mother, yet our relationships and experiences of her were quite different. What he recalled and appreciated most was her strength in standing up to Dad's "old-fashioned" ways and expectations—the beauty in her imperfection. For years, I focused on—and judged her for—her shortcomings. When I became a mother myself, it opened up a well of appreciation that she had loved us unconditionally, as she had never been loved.

16

I was a child around six years old. One Sunday, our family, including an aunt and uncle, gathered at a slightly splintered picnic table on a cement patio. A quiet girl, I observed a lot. Noticed body language and faces. I sat a few plastic chairs away from the grown-ups, in front of a towering plate of home-cooked brisket.

They spoke Yiddish, unintelligible to my ears. It was not understood by my mother-from-Newark, either. When she couldn't take it anymore, she protested, and the conversation resumed in English. To me, Yiddish was incomprehensible background noise; it gave me a sense of being left out for my own good.

But what registered was Aunt Piri's wrinkled pale blue blouse sleeves rolled above her fleshy elbows as her forearms rested on the table. Was it the first time I noticed?

I stared at my aunt's forearm, where a row of numbers in faded ink reminded me of the stamped chicken skins in my uncle's butcher shop. Instinctively, I knew enough not to ask her at the picnic table about the numbers. These things were not discussed. The War was never discussed.

I waited until the car ride home to ask my father.

As if talking about the price of chickens last week, he answered without emotion, "In the camps, the Nazis used this as a way of tracking prisoners. But only at the start. It got so that there were too many people arriving to stamp arms, so the Nazis stopped. I arrived at the camp after her; there were too many of us. I did not get a number stamp."

I thought, Aunt Piri has to wake up each day, the numbers burning her eyes like a fresh reminder of hell. No wonder I never heard her laugh.

An "American" cousin on Mom's side played the harp. Her brother, the piano. Their father, my uncle, played the xylophone. My aunt was the family eccentric with a beehive bun piled high upon her head. These were *The Fancy* relatives.

Guests invited to their home perched on silk chairs and listened to music salon-style. Hired help served meals on fragile china. My parents were occasionally invited. For me, going there felt like being in a movie; it was so different from how we lived.

Years later, Dad revealed to me that, other than he and my mother, the adults there were all *highly educated*. He said, "I listened to one dinner guest speak of how proud he was of his son for his professional accomplishments. All I could focus on was the father bankrolled his son, who also benefited from his guidance and support. It didn't seem a spectacular or independent accomplishment to me. His son had all that help."

What was I picking up from that perspective of his? The value of making it on one's own was the only way that mattered? The diminished value in his view—that became mine too—of making it any other way?

To put his comment in context, Dad received the news that his father, Jacob, died of pneumonia in January 1945. Although interred at the same sprawling concentration camp, they were separated, so Dad wasn't with Jacob when he died. At age fifteen, he was a fatherless boy, without parental guidance for how to navigate his life. This loss fueled a fierce value of self-reliance. It also created a deep wellspring of sorrow.

17

Trauma is stored. Freud's contemporary Carl Jung believed that what remains unconscious does not dissolve, but rather resurfaces in our lives as fate or fortune. "Whatever does not emerge as Consciousness," he said, "returns as Destiny." In other words, we're likely to keep repeating our unconscious patterns until we bring them into the light of awareness. Both Jung and Freud noted that whatever is too difficult to process does not fade away on its own, but rather is stored in our unconscious.

The core trauma for our family was murder—innocent lives targeted for slaughter, snuffing out with them hopes and dreams. False, dangerous narratives were amplified, spread, and repeated by those in power. If they were not complicit, bystanders looked the other way- remained silent, indifferent, spectators. Marty was mostly silent while Jeff and I were growing up about what and who went missing from his life.

In those days, we rarely spoke of the Holocaust by name. It hung, like a sprawling attic web, in the air. My questions remained unasked for fear of causing more pain, for wanting, needing, to know about the *life that came before.* We vowed to "never forget" what happened en masse to the six million but had no particular knowledge about our own family.

That came much later.

18

A n avid reader, I devoured published efforts of *real writers.* I relegated the task of *the story* to others while my own churned inside. I admired authors who can write what they mean in a way that expressed what I feel but could not put to words. It was, to me, a most courageous, sacred act to be vulnerable in that way. Perhaps this was why I waited sixty years to do so. I told myself, *I don't know how, I'm not ready yet, what if I put the effort in and it fails, what if what I write is a betrayal of those I love?*

BIRD SONG

Is it courage or urgency?
That brings me to this point of setting on fire story upon story
Tales of my childhood, unsaddling life of a heavy load, not meant for carrying alone.
Gone is the obedient girl
Who internalized loyalty, privacy, believed she had a right to only so much joy in the world

Born a daughter, I emerge as a mother, advocate for how
*   we will live*
I want to shout it and spread it from way up high
Wisdom born of age and brave, yes
Though mostly it comes down to
Making life count, especially the ordinary moments,
We are the lucky ones. We who are here. We get to choose
*   how we live now.*
Not everyone gets to hear the first bluebird sing of spring.

19

"You ARE our LIFE," Mom assured me often. Rather than being a comfort or confidence builder, as she may have intended, the assurance felt like an enormous weight. She heaped praise upon me. No act too insignificant for notice. Due to her upbringing, she lacked confidence, and it became the one ingredient she deemed necessary to live a happy life. Her mission in life was to ensure that, unlike her, I didn't lack confidence. However, her generous yet generalized praise often had the opposite effect: I struggled to decipher or trust sincere praise, and I learned to distrust compliments as mostly hollow gestures.

Apparently, I couldn't muster the courage to deny her, to say, "No, thank you; I'm not deserving of blanket praise." I view it now as a way to see that the daughter she and Dad raised—good student, dutiful, seemingly at home in her own skin, was a tribute and miraculous result of their unlikely survival and union.

Middle-school peers taught me how to smoke, drink, and ditch my brain. It wasn't easy at first, but at fourteen, I began taking my cues from the popular girls, with whom I would never fit in. I stopped talking about books and speaking up in class—being a smart girl in middle school wasn't cool. Smart girls were labeled "nerds" and that peer designation meant social suicide. How I appeared to others then, was everything. In longing to belong, I lost myself.

In middle school, for the first time in my life, I rebelled and hard. My grades tanked. I cut school and got suspended by my French teacher for smoking cigarettes on school property—all for social recognition and acceptance by the "in" crowd.

The occasion also marked the first time I chose to be identified as separate from my family. To rebel. Went willingly from sweet to snarly, compliant to combative. I knew of no other way to break free, to declare myself independent from my parents, and what seemed to be impossibly high expectations of me. So I literally and figuratively stuck out my hitchhiker's thumb and tried to get miles away—from them, their pasts, my obedient nature.

Messages I received in middle-school culture were clear: Don't be smart. Don't do better or want more for yourself. In my willingness to blend, in my quest to belong, I diminished myself, staying small and indifferent like the others.

One time I chose to shine, I nearly lost my two best friends. We were at a battle of the bands' event at the local church, and one of the band members invited us back to his parents' basement to hear the band practice after the show. They asked which of us wanted to take the microphone to sing Led Zeppelin's "Stairway to Heaven."

I held back, watched both friends eagerly grab the mic.

"How about you?" a band member asked when they finished, pointing at me.

Reluctantly, I stood at the mic and sang, very self-consciously, what was then my favorite song. After the last note faded away, a band member offered me, only me, a chance to sing with the band. The car ride home with my friends was as stonily silent as midnight is dark. They didn't talk to me for days. My teenage self memorized a lesson: Do not stand out if you want to fit in.

When I entered college as an English major and psychology minor, I immersed myself in poetry, literature, and the social sciences. What breathed inside me, an irrepressible desire to learn, was cultivated and coaxed into expression. In higher learning, the peer-scorn I had experienced in public school for using my brain no longer existed. Quite the opposite: Curiosity and education were encouraged.

I felt free.

20

In a considerable departure from my father's Orthodox upbringing, religion didn't play a traditional role in our family, other than celebrating major Jewish holidays. My father worked on Friday night, so we didn't keep Shabbat. I avoided reading books or watching movies about World War II, though the fear of knowing the horrors of it was buried in my DNA. Avoidance was, essentially, our religion.

During my sophomore year in college, a movie called *The Garden of the Finzi-Continis* played in the campus theater.

I asked my non-Jewish boyfriend to see it with me. The lights dimmed, and we held hands in the darkened theater. We shared an oversized, buttered bag of popcorn. The story played out on screen, and I became aware of holding my breath. Midway through the film, all the air was sucked from my lungs. I thought of Dad as a 14-year-old—separated from family, not knowing who was dead or alive, subject to abject cruelty, haunted daily by fear, disease, and death.

I wrenched my hand from my boyfriend's, darted up the unlit aisle, and fled the theater, only stopping when I got to the campus fountain. Tears poured down my cheeks.

My boyfriend caught up with me. "What is it? What's wrong?" his voice pleading, face full of concern.

My chest heaved. I could not stop sobbing. It was there, perched on the edge of the cold concrete fountain wall in winter. That was when I decided to claim my story.

Between bouts of sobbing, I revealed what little I knew about my father's and my family's past. My emotions ripped my insides raw. Though I trusted him with my secret, and he held me close, it dawned on me that he did not understand—and that I could not expect that of him.

He was raised Episcopal with a father of German descent. I learned that Jews were not admitted to their country club. College had brought us together, and we bumped up against our identities. Until that moment, I had not processed what happened before my birth. What had been suppressed and unspoken was, in fact, *inseparable* from me. I confronted that truth now. Though I appeared as someone strong, my core vulnerability—the truth of who I was—had been mostly invisible, especially to myself. It would be decades before it became nationally visible— when Dad was a guest of honor at the White House.

Because our family had minimized the impact of our legacy wound, being invited by President Obama and Michelle Obama to celebrate at their annual Chanukah party felt a little ironic.

A Czech menorah had been discovered, and the White House sought Czech Holocaust survivors for their event. As a former Czech citizen and Holocaust Survivor, Marty had been invited to be a guest of honor, and I was his fortunate plus one.

Being invited to the White House was a new level of being witnessed for Marty. And he was humbled and grateful. We, along with a few others, first had a private audience with the president and first lady. We posed for photos. I talked gardening with Michelle when I overheard an exchange between Marty and the president.

"Thank you, Mr. President," I heard Marty say.

President Obama said, "No. Thank YOU. For being an inspiration."

In his public remarks that evening, President Obama referenced Nelson Mandela and Marty in the same sentence. The large room overflowed with celebrities, Supreme Court Justices, and other luminaries. But the only thing that mattered to me that night was the recognition my father received, on behalf of what he, his family, and all the other victims experienced.

21

TRUE SONG

I have recurring dreams
Of waiting for my turn.
In line, at work, for a lift.
I've invested heavily in waiting
My turn,
Sequestered in silence
My one true song,
My story. Is it mine to tell? Where will I find the courage?
    How to possibly tell it true?
Not knowing,
My story is stillbirth, pages between notebook covers.
Decades of journals gasp for air in a nondescript box,
    silver dust on top.
Imprisoned with heavy-duty duct tape,
Pages, once written, never opened–until now.

22

What breaks my heart is life unexpressed. I have suffered under "the spell of keeping it all in." Yet— dare I call it suffering?

23

Marty's larger than life-size image became one of thirty-eight survivor portraits created by Italian photographer Luigi Toscano. The outdoor exhibit has traveled its way around the world.

Marty and I arrived for the official unveiling ceremony on a chilly spring day. As we walked down the steps to the National Mall, a swath of green space in the center of Washington, D.C., the enormous scale and scope of the project became visible. I paused to take it in from a distance.

Our chairs sat overlooking the National Mall reflective pool, our backs to the looming statue of President Lincoln. This monument, the first I visited when I moved to D.C. in my twenties. This location, a place I've paced, peddled, jogged, and photographed. This historic landmark, appreciated by tourists as well as locals.

Remarks were made by the USHMM Director, German Embassy officials, and the artist.

"Be present," I told myself. I didn't know what to expect. After the program, I took my father's elbow, led him away from the guided tour, to find his portrait. We strolled past portraits of other survivors flanking the reflecting pool. Some he recognized. Finally, we came upon his.

I gazed upon the oversized photograph. Marty's face was weathered, older than the face I knew. His eyes reflected the saddest sad, blue Danube deep. I thought, "I would surely have been swallowed whole if I knew all of how he suffered."

I turned to watch him observe his portrait. He looked away.

"I see an old man," he said, decidedly detached.

"Let me take your photo," I said, waving him closer to the display.

A family of four paused near us before continuing past. On instinct, I ran to catch up with them. They were tourists from Greece.

"Want to see something interesting?" I asked their school-age daughter. "See that man?" I pointed at Marty. "That portrait is of him."

They exchanged words among themselves in rapid-fire Greek before expressing their surprise to me in English and continuing on their way.

But before we were out of earshot, their teenage son called to us, "Excuse me, may I take a picture with you, sir?" He, too, acted on instinct and to document the moment, memorialize living history. Larger than life, larger than any of us.

24

Growing up, there was not a woman I knew who lived a life that worked for them. My impression was that mothers I knew felt silenced and trapped. As a girl, I wondered, "Why can't I see from anyone's example how I can live a full life beyond motherhood and wifely duties?" It was a question I frequently pondered in my journal. I ached for a female role model who could help me find my way.

In one of Dad's sisters, Celia, I detected elegance and intelligence, the likes of which I had not seen in other women I knew. Well dressed and well-spoken, she was Dad's older sister, who attended gymnasium (high school) before the war. She had been in Auschwitz and Bergen-Belsen with her mother and sisters when they died. My father looked up to Celia and her high regard for education.

What I observed of her didn't square with what I later learned, that of discontentment with her traditional female role in life. She was ambitious and smart in her own right. Though she appreciated being privileged by most postwar immigrants' standards, she pined for a purpose that was hers alone, not a byproduct of wifedom and motherhood.

From my earliest memories, I imagined what it would be like if she were my mother. When I became a mother, I sometimes imagined what she would say to me, especially at times when I felt the privilege of discontent, tending my family's garden, but not a purpose of my own.

25

I decided at fifteen that I wanted a real job, to work for someone else, doing anything other than work for my father or someone he knew. A new mall had opened near our home and seemed like the perfect place for me to earn real money. I asked my mother to drop me off so I could apply for jobs.

The legal minimum age to get a work permit was sixteen. When working for a family business, those laws didn't apply. Not only did my birth certificate betray me, but I also looked younger than I was. Undeterred, I practiced saying that my birth date was one year earlier. Doing so was wrong, I knew, but I rationalized that I needed money. My ruse worked, and soon I was serving hot dogs, soda, and ice cream to hungry mall cruisers.

Having learned at my father's knee about hard work and customer service, I soon had my work hours fully booked for after school and weekends. I burned the candle at both ends, running to keep up with homework and my snack-shop schedule. I came to despise the scent of boiled hot dogs and grew tired of the guessing game the employees played to keep boredom at bay, where we'd predict what a customer would order. Within four months, I ended up in the hospital for a week with pneumonia. And my snack-shop gig came to a screeching halt.

26

Marty's first effort at public speaking was shaky, disjointed, rote. Regardless of an unsophisticated delivery, while he spoke, the auditorium was silent as a country road at midnight. During the more harrowing passages of his Holocaust recollections, those assembled heaved a communal gasp.

Marty's hand shook, rattling the notes he held tight. He kept his eyes on what he'd written. I knew within the first few sentences he uttered that he wasn't holding back, releasing anguish with sorrow so overwhelming it wailed, despite the uncertain delivery. He spoke about days of being crammed into filthy and dark train cattle cars with fellow captives, not knowing where they were headed.

Finally, the train containing his family arrived at Auschwitz. Tall men in pressed uniforms brandished guns and *bully* sticks. German Shepherds strained at their leashes, barking and snarling at the newly arrived prisoners. Mayhem ensued, and angry shouts ordered them to get in line.

Marty tried to join his mother and younger sisters to take care of them.

"You can't go over there!" an angry guard yelled and forced Marty to leave them and get into another line.

By morning, Marty's mother, Golda, and youngest sisters, Esther and Miriam, had already been gassed. Hannah and Celia were sent to Bergen-Belsen, where Hannah perished. Celia survived and was liberated from there.

As he spoke in front of strangers, my father cried, his voice cracking like the glass of so many store windows on Kristallnacht. Shards of memory punctured wounds never before aired or healed. Despite his apparent distress, he soldiered on.

He spoke of the day the Hungarians came to arrest his family. "I could not get it out of my mind, the worry about what will happen to the calf with its skin smooth to my touch? And my favorite horse whose bare back carried me on errands dependably? It took a while to banish worry about who would care for them while we were gone."

Much to our relief, he not only made it through his speech but experienced an emotional release in the process. It became the first of hundreds of presentations where his story brought entire audiences to their feet, clapping. They rooted for him. They wanted him to be okay. They cared. He connected because of his authenticity, the vulnerability of an open heart. He refused to gloss over his pain for their sake and no longer attempted to hide, to keep himself separate and safe.

After he finished, I watched strangers line up to approach him, asking for his autograph. As if he were holy, they wanted to touch him, hug him close. It was beautiful and moving. The intensity was also unsettling—it created an illusion of intimacy and understanding that seemed impossible after listening to him speak for an hour. Yet, they have traveled a chapter of his story and glimpsed at his ability to remain human in the face of evil. They have sipped from his never-empty cup of hope.

Marty expressed surprise that his story moved others.

27

I was named after Marty's mother, Golda, which in Yiddish means *gold*. He spoke of his mother in superlatives, recalled from the tender age at which he last knew her.

"She was the best mother and the best cook. How she managed it all—raising a large family, tending to the house and farm, serving meals for extra income to those passing through town and to workers—I will never know," Marty says. "She always told me I was her most difficult child—of nine! Too fussy about what I wore and what I ate."

Golda kept a small garden separate and apart from the acres overseen by her husband. In it, she planted root vegetables like radishes and potatoes, staples to get her large family through the winter. I imagined her wearing a black homemade skirt, possibly itchy, fencing off "a room of her own," in agrarian terms. There would have been no sense of privacy or chance for rest from the relentless demands of farm and family on her. I like to think that the patch of her own gave her a sense of sovereignty and accomplishment.

One story that stayed with me is how, during the war, Golda gathered her daughters to prepare food, which Marty then delivered to a non-Jewish neighbor who helped feed a Jewish child hiding in their attic. Golda's compassion demonstrated that she would willingly part with precious rations and subject her children to a degree of risk to save one life. In those days, compassion was punishable by death. Kindness was a radical act.

I am reminded of Golda as Marty honors tradition by delivering his own homemade soup (alternating between bean, pea, potato, and cherry) and meals to family members and friends. Nourishment as connection—homemade love.

Recently, my cousin showed me the only photograph that exists of Golda. She appears to be about seventeen in the undated, black-and-white image. She was seated, milk-white hands resting one atop the other, her neck long and lean. The long, flowering gown she wore modestly covered her arms and legs. What struck me most were her deep-set dark eyes and mouth, which gave her a serious air. She was probably married to Jacob by then. My uncle Mendel carried that photo with him throughout the war when he was in the Russian army. This single photograph is the only surviving image of the large family we lost.

28

When he was almost ninety, Marty decided to take a trip to Ohio for what would be a demanding two-day schedule of three speaking engagements and hosted meals. My brother and I tried in vain to dissuade him. He insisted. I knew this was proof he needed that he was not past his prime, that his message was not snuffed out.

"I'm a simple person," he said to me during a phone call from Ohio, "And they treat me like a celebrity." He sounded ecstatic. "Over 800 people were at one of the events!"

When he returned home, he recounted that the dinner hostess for one of the Ohio events had a friend named Knish. "Like the puffed pastry baked brown that surrounds potato filling. *Knish*," he repeated over and over, the skin around his eyes wrinkling as tears pooled into them with delight. "And then, guess what? A guest walks in with knishes. Can you imagine?" he says. "Her name was Knish, a potato puff."

I'd rarely seen him laugh like that. My mother used to tell me no one in his family laughs because of how they suffered. That she wished Dad laughed with her more. In sharing the story of *knish*, he laughed to the point of doubling over.

Most people are inherently good, was his frequent refrain. Long ago, he decided to trust others when he could have chosen to rage or retreat. Courage to do so was not a given for a survivor. Facing demons of the past, he showed up for the hard truth and said no to silencing his voice any longer.

29

When I was eight years old, my best friend's next-door neighbor, a boy a year older than us, came up behind me as I left my classroom after school. Bright orange construction-paper pumpkins adorned the third-grade classroom windows.

"Hey, you!" a boy's voice called.

As I turned around, he rushed at me, pushing me roughly against the classroom corner's rough cement bricks. My eyes darted around. We were the only ones around.

His dark eyes glared with rage, and his jaw was set tight. He growled, "I didn't know you were Jewish. You. You killed Jesus."

I felt his hot breath on my face, and, for a split second, I thought he might bite me. "No," I whispered before falling silent, hoping his unchecked anger would thaw. The air was filled with his venom, and once it was spent, he left me quaking in the corner. I knew I would never tell my parents, vowing to myself to protect my father from pain—a conscious act on my part to avoid adding pain and suffering to a barely bearable load. So strong was the unconscious obedience to the family legacy of silence, I kept the story under wraps until I began to write this book.

30

Marty was a hero. Strangers, relatives, and friends repeatedly told me so. Surely, my mind insisted, there was no room for two heroes in one family, especially when one was lucky enough to survive a death camp and immigrate to America?

How dare I ask for more? Eager to please, following an inner script to play it small and safe, I couldn't see how I could be a hero in my own life. Besides, as a wife and mother, I had family duties to consider. My mother and grandmothers hadn't figured that one out; neither had my aunts. Was it even possible for me to forge another way?

31

We were shocked to receive news that, at seventy-five, Marty was selected to run with the Winter Olympic Torch along the streets near the USHMM in Washington, D.C. Aspiring to go the distance, he doubled down on his early morning gym regimen. Wishing to be of emotional support, Mom invited my family over before the big day.

She'd created a Marty Museum of sorts by decorating their home with memorabilia from his speaking engagements—wall-to-wall awards, posters, commemorations, and taped letters from people all over the world who had heard him speak.

That day, there was a new exhibit. Hanging from the stereo cabinet was Marty's uniform, a white runner's suit emblazoned with shades of periwinkle, a Salt Lake City 2002 Olympic Torch Relay badge on the upper left (above the heart). His sneakers, soft white gloves, and a white woven cap that also sported the Olympic insignia sat on the parquet floor beneath. Long underwear (still in the package) lay beside them. It was surreal–this man who had been a victim of history would have an honor that few Americans experience—and in the nation's capital.

We researched the history of the torch relay and its significance. The tradition began in the Ancient Greek Olympics and was revived at the 1936 Berlin Games. In 2002, the relay was a sixty-five-day run, lasting from December 4, 2001, to February 8, 2002, which carried the Olympic flame through Washington, D.C., and forty-six of America's fifty states. The flame itself symbolizes "the light of spirit, knowledge, and life."

Marty's leg of running with the torch occurred at the end of December. We gathered with our young children, our close friends, and their children on the coldest, bitterest winter night any of us could remember. Bundled in winter coats, ski gloves, and toasty hats, we planned to walk quickly alongside him for his entire leg. Waiting together, we jumped up and down, not only from excitement but to try to stay warm.

The torch weighed four point four pounds and measured thirty-three inches. Marty received the torch from the relay runner, and he was off. And so were we, our eyes on him. We watched with reverence as he held the torch high. Not all heroes wear capes—Marty wore long underwear and a running suit.

To this day, I don't know if it was the adrenaline or the freezing temperatures, but our group of young parents and young children struggled to keep up with Marty. That's how fast he ran, carrying the torch high and proud.

It was clear, watching him, seeing all the media and the pressing crowds cheering him on, that his example was what we all needed, a life-affirming shot in the arm. He suffered the worst of humanity. Yet he lived his life, and taught us to live ours, with integrity and kindness. With an always burning flame of hope. No doubt, that hope has played a part in my managing to dig deep and go public with my writing. Just as that proud public display of who Marty is on a bitterly cold night is a heartwarming tribute to him, fellow survivors, and those who were lost, my story carries memories that burn bright for grandchildren, their children, and all who hear our story.

32

My mother's life was, in some ways, shrink-wrapped, which conjures *The Store's* state-of-the-art shrink wrap machine. As directed, we'd pull tightly with two hands to remove excess air when packaging meat or cold cuts, so we limited exposure to air and movement. Mom's driving excursions were limited to local roads and a few exits along the parkway. She mostly lived life at home and had few friends. She was often sad. I could tell from how her lips scrunched together like knotted twine that defied her perky orange lipstick.

Many women in the neighborhood were home alone in the daytime when children were at school and husbands at work. The women dealt with their isolation in various ways. Some drank or took valium. My friend Karen's mother was always "out," so mostly we hung out at her house in our young teens.

One afternoon, as I returned home from the library where I was doing homework, I spotted Karen's mother crossing Main Street. It was the middle of the day. I paused to observe her, noting the red miniskirt and high-heeled shoes she wore. They were the color of cherry licorice and made her hips sway. Hair was done-up high, dyed blonder than blond. She had someplace to go, and it wasn't to work or to meet a friend for shopping.

I mentioned it to a friend of mine.

"She's having an affair," my friend said.

"Huh?" I said.

"Haven't you noticed before, the way she walks and dresses and acts? She's out to meet a man. And it's not her bore of a husband."

33

Marty, the butcher who sliced cold cuts by day, turned pages by night. My father was a scholar. Despite being robbed of formal schooling beyond eighth grade, he taught me to love learning for its own sake. In the process, he imparted a recipe for living well, where words and quality ingredients are essential.

Every word Dad didn't know, he scribbled into a spiral-bound notepad, the blue ink leaking from the ballpoint pen he favored, staining his fingers. He'd look up definitions in the dictionary, writing them down next to the words, committing to memory as he wrote.

Mornings before heading to The Store, Dad read. Often, he scoured the Encyclopedia Brittanica, one of his proudest purchases (the other, his stereo system), trying to quench his thirst for knowledge.

To learn English, Dad read the local paper front to back, listened to the news, and had a hardcover library book at the ready. He spoke achingly about others who were "educated." Growing up, I perceived the only time he felt "less than" was next to someone who had a degree.

Willingness to learn helped him start a business and exposed him to other viewpoints.

At some point, Mom wanted to throw away some of Dad's encyclopedias, to make room for what I can't recall. I defended his right to keep those books because his enthusiasm for learning was housed on shelves, contained between those pocked ivory hardcovers stamped with green letters. To me, those books were his diploma.

34

When I was a kid, parents using a belt to discipline their children was the norm in my neighborhood. Vivid memories raise recollections of tall skinny neighbor boys in their PJs or white Fruit of the Looms, screaming, running around their house perimeters to escape the rage of their fathers.

When I went against her wishes as a teenager, Mom used to make threats like, "Wait till your father gets home." In my teens, most transgressions related to my sassy mouth. When I didn't agree with her, I talked back. Other times, I broke curfew (I was one of the few who had to be home by midnight) or was caught in a lie (about whom I was with or where I was hanging out). There were times when she took matters into her own hands, which usually involved forcing a slick bar of Ivory soap into my mouth.

I hated it when she threatened me with Dad's wrath to come; hated her. My father did not favor hitting to make a point. Instead, he would reason with me. With my brother, not so much—their disagreements often meant shouting and resulted in impasse.

Except for once, when I was fifteen. Mom caught two of my friends and me hitchhiking. She happened to drive by when my thumb was up, poised, in search of a ride. Mom insisted that Dad "give it to me, but good."

The spanking happened in the basement, with its mildew odor and bright fluorescent lights radiating disapproval. Marty said, "I have to do it. It hurts me as much as it hurts you," and *wham!* my backside got walloped. It hurt. But the shock of its happening to me was worse. How much risk-taking was worth it? It would take years to find out.

35

When I was fifty-nine years old, I signed people up to vote. Even though I lived in the metro Washington, D.C. area, I never saw myself as political. I went door to door in unfamiliar neighborhoods, across the state line. Conversations with strangers were often, though not always, amicable.

At one house, an elderly man invited me into his home. His stooped form shuffled into his dining room so he could sit while I helped him register for an absentee ballot. His wife lay in the next room, infirm and confined to her bed, an aide by her side.

A long row of framed family photos, along with letters and cards, lined a section of the wall equal to the full length of the dining room table. What a privilege to be let into this man's world, if only for a few moments. A man whose light and love for extended family shone so brightly under what appeared to be trying circumstances. He cared, about people and politics, however infirm he may have been.

Just like Marty. The wind filling my sails, or so I assumed. I counted on Marty's judgment. And as he entered his ninth decade, his well-meaning advice became, at times, questionable. Watching this natural change take place as a result of aging undid me at unexpected times.

He never taught me to bat a ball or balance a checkbook. Instead, he taught me how to rely on myself to navigate a life that, in many ways, was not fair or just. To treat everyone equally. To not be a victim. To not strive for less because I was female. To be independent. Marty urged me to go bigger—to try out for student newspaper and yearbook editor, as an officer on student council, to go away to college, to stand up for myself and what I believe in. All the things he never had the chance to do.

Who will I be when I lose him? He whose cooking has nourished me, aromas that wafted down a long hallway of experiences that fortified me like air? He whose kindness and wisdom braised my impatience through the toughest of times? The prospect feels like too much to bear. In the end, I know I'll be a stronger woman having marinated and grown with his values.

36

When I was in college, the chance to learn from empowered female professors presented itself, and I was ready for role models full of knowledge. Course materials in feminist literature and poetry deepened my understanding of how the world worked. I craved an environment where learning, opinion, and expression were the mission.

I made new friends. Their parents held different positions than the adults I already knew. Their parents were mostly educated and well-to-do. Many were in Who's Who directories, CEOs of corporations, owners of companies. Although my upbringing was different, I no longer felt the need to hide who I was; in fact, I was writing lots of poetry that seemed to pour out of me from the angst of love relationships, a tragic death on campus, inequality, and insincere people.

I believed with everything I knew that words and bigger constructs were to be ingested, digested, savored. They allowed me to inhale the salt air of freedom, of knowing more than I had experienced on journeys through books. The time came for both Marty and me to transition from passive to active voice. He would do so in his way, and I, in mine. But the pursuit would be the same: to grow ourselves by growing others with what we understand at our core: our own stories. By relaying them, we make them count— our stories matter. And so does yours.

37

When Marty was fourteen, his family was rounded up from Hungary's Munkács ghetto and transported by cattle car to Auschwitz, where he and his family were first imprisoned. More than fifty years later, Marty was asked to be included in a United States Holocaust Museum student trip for the March of Remembrance to Auschwitz.

One of the museum chaperones, Betsy, said to me, "I was surprised that he'd want to return to Auschwitz so soon after beginning his volunteering at the museum. I wondered if we were doing the right thing by bringing him with us and worried that we might re-traumatize him."

The plane from Dulles landed at Krakow, after a long flight. Understandably, Marty's anxiety ratcheted up the closer the plane got to arrival. Betsy and her fellow chaperone worried.

The group gathered around the luggage carousel, watching it go round and round. When it became clear that his suitcase was lost, Marty turned to the person next to him and said, "Funny...this is what happened the last time I came to Poland!" His humor defused a tense situation, and the students dubbed him *Lost Luggage Marty*.

Marty was grouped with students from a Catholic college and befriended the other chaperone, a nun. The students and trip leaders all fell in love with Marty. He found himself constantly surrounded by others. As the groups toured Krakow and Warsaw, he spoke to and taught all the ones he encountered.

Betsy said, "The highlight was watching him return to Auschwitz. He showed incredible vulnerability simply on the physical return to Auschwitz. Everyone compassionately honored his need for space to grieve, and those who witnessed him reciting the Kaddish to commemorate his family were especially moved. My worries were for nothing. I watched him become a real leader on that trip."

38

My father and his wardrobe! Marty showed up for a doctor appointment wearing navy cotton work pants that survived hundreds of wash cycles over at least fifty years—the same pants he wore to work in The Store. Now stained and too baggy for him, the pants fit a younger Marty, who weighed more and did 100 push-ups on the living room floor every morning before work. It was a habit developed during his stint in the American army when he served as a corporal in the Korean War.

After the appointment, I broached the delicate subject of his wearing old clothes.

He replied, as he always did, "But I like these pants. I found them in the back of my closet, and they still fit, and they were fine when I bought them in a private men's store." He paused. "And they don't make pants of this quality anymore."

I knew he needed to say that. He needed me to hear him say that. We sat in silence until he relented. "Okay," he said. "I didn't realize how they looked. If you tell me they don't look good anymore, I'll only wear them around the house from now on."

My mother, may she rest in peace, would have wanted that. He could be stubbornly persistent, we knew. But he cared about others too, about their and our reactions and feelings—enough to change his mind.

39

Family dinner was a given—every night, except Friday, at 6:30, Joan had a homemade meal on the table as Marty walked through the door. Even in my teenage years, sitting down for dinner together was unquestioned.

Supper was an unrushed event, a time when everyone shared details about their day. Sometimes tempers flared. Regardless of our financial circumstances, we always ate well. Dad stocked premium grade meats, fish, and groceries at *The Store*. He "shopped" from Mom's list and brought home fresh dinner ingredients every night. Meals included filet mignon, sloppy joes, fish, and pasta. Canned and frozen meals—shortcuts, Dad considered them demons— were not allowed.

When I became a mother, I consciously continued this tradition of nourishing stomachs to pepper the family with a sense of grounding and belonging at mealtime. Dinners weren't always peaceful. But they were always a safe, dependable harbor. One change made to the routine established by my parents happened by encouraging my children to invite their friends, which expanded the circle. My husband and I welcomed our friends, too, especially to join in the Shabbat ritual on Friday nights. At my husband's prompting, we started Friday night dinners when our two children were in elementary school and continued the tradition while they lived at home.

When our daughter was in her twenties, she told me, "Friday night dinner was one of the things I treasure most about growing up."

40

For spending money, I turned to cocktail waitressing in my late teens and continued the gig throughout college. My parents did not want me to waitress, but I prevailed with the truth—I needed the spending money. I enjoyed the income, but working for tips in bars required steely emotional separation and armor. It was common for male customers to grab, grope, propose, and drool when, and even before, they drank. Some tugged at my bra strap, reached for me when they shouldn't have. Sometimes I'd make large tips. Other times, people drank all night and left me nothing.

One night, the big boss, who people in town said was in the Mob, summoned me to his penthouse above the restaurant. He wanted to meet the new waitress alone. A few female co-workers warned me that I had no choice but to go.

"He'll close the door behind you before making a pass," they said.

When the summons came, I felt bile rise in my throat. Although I knew it was wrong of him to ask, I never considered that "no, I'm not going up there alone" was an option if I wanted to keep my job. In my upbringing, short of mortal danger, one did what one was asked by those in authority. Although my parents spoke plenty about what distinguished right from wrong, they didn't so much when it came to making waves and questioning those in power.

And so I went, standing as close to the door as possible. Barely looking at the boss, I responded in flat tones to imply disinterest to questions and observations about my appearance. Fortunately, nothing happened. I rationalized I would survive being a waitress but felt a red hot flush of shame that made it hard to deny I was enduring being objectified in the role of waitressing, which was a different matter entirely.

I was eighteen years old. I handled the situation on my own. I kept silent.

41

WAITRESS, UNMASKED

many a customer
shall assume
    this woman has a tray of gold,
bearing
    booze. butts. breasts
available for a price.

for a quarter
the juke will play
    a beat, a line—
pinchy pinchy
    find a lady
hanky panky
    do it quickie.

i don't want to
f**k you
    mister

down your fifth
johnny walker
  and rock on.

which is brightest?
  the strobes
    the coins
      or his eyes
pulling at my skirt
slit
  like a zipper?

oh, say
  can you see
    past this smile
down deep
  into pride.

                    Written in Ithaca, New York, May 1980

42

The house plants of my childhood were plastic. Manufactured. Man-made. Mom adored decorative plastics—the fruit, artichokes, tulips, and roses that adorned tops of cabinets and tables. The way Dad later explained it, while Mom loved greenery, and tended plants outside, she did not want the ongoing responsibility of watering a house full of plants.

We briefly had a house cleaner. One day after she'd been at our home, we noticed water puddled on the hallway linoleum around the base of a houseplant. It dawned on us that the cleaner had watered the plant. Who could blame her? After all, who keeps a house full of plastic plants, fruits, and vegetables? Next time she came, Mom held the woman's hand to the iridescent green leaf to illustrate why it needn't be watered. Soon, the cleaner stopped coming. My love for the authentic grew more deeply rooted.

43

One Sunday, instead of spending time with Dad's relatives, my parents, my brother, and I went on an adventure. We drove along winding roads beneath fall foliage. Dad was visibly energized. More chatty than usual. We were going horseback riding in Watchung, New Jersey.

Mom said, "Your father loves riding. He's very good at it."

Dad recounted how, when he was growing up, his family always had two or three horses at a time. He recalled a particular mare he enjoyed riding bareback. "There's nothing quite like the freedom of galloping through the countryside," he said.

Picture my father, then in midlife, mounted on a high chestnut steed, heel-kicking the horse into action. We watched as it threw its head up, mane flying, and galloped off into the distance with Dad gripping the reins and saddle horn for dear life.

It was the last time Marty climbed atop a saddle to ride free through the pines. He learned, in this case, to leave the past in the past.

44

As a child, sometimes I crept into my parents' bedroom to survey the contents of their drawers for clues about them. It seemed to be the room where secrets were kept, and I was a curious girl. I discovered inside my father's walnut dresser a drawer full of ironed white hankies, stacked and folded with precision. When asked why he assembled them into neat white hanky towers, he replied, "Because I'm not an animal." Was his insistence for cleaniness and order of his things, with the sense of dignity it gave him, a consequence not only of his upbringing but also of the concentration camps?

45

In the camps, it was safest to be silent. To speak up was to be exposed to cruelty, judgment, even death. Were it not for the slight-framed Marty wearing sacks of rocks stuffed under a tattered overcoat, were it not for an SS officer shouting at him to separate from his mother and sisters on the selection line, neither he nor my brother and I would be here. Not to mention his four grandchildren. He always said how unlikely it was that it was he, not his older, stronger brothers, who survived.

Marty lived with the daily threat of death for more than eighteen months, emerging with his humanity intact. He learned to compartmentalize the past, pragmatic about the present, and certain about one thing in the future: Once he became a parent, he didn't want his children to grow up with hate. The weight of survival, though, became the breath he inhaled, sadness its exhale.

Almost everywhere Marty spoke, an audience member asked him about the role religious faith played in his survival. I believe they expected him to say he prayed, that he believed, and that's what got him through. Publicly, he tread lightly and respectfully around the topic.

Privately, he told me of his moment of reckoning with God, of being with his father and a small group of religious male prisoners. They gathered on a hilltop at Mauthausen concentration camp, the blistering sun beating down on their spent and undernourished bodies. They recited ritual Jewish prayers for the holiday of Sukkot, the festival of the harvest.

A boy of just fourteen, Marty surveyed the prison, which was not fit for animals. The recent death "showers" of his mother and sisters in chambers flooded with Zykon B gas, the loss of the family home and property, and the decimation of their community fresh in his memory. He turned and walked away in disgust and disbelief. He recalled, "God deserted us. We were treated worse than animals, left for dead and dying."

While Marty was schooled in orthodoxy and always identified as Jewish, after the war, he did not live in a Jewish community and would never again practice with the wholehearted conviction of his childhood. So, when he immigrated to the states and chose to live in a predominantly Catholic community, he deemed it safest to remain silent about his past.

For me, too, fitting into my hometown, a place without the knowledge of or curiosity about the Holocaust, meant hiding my family's history. No one told me, but I never said a word. What had that silence cost me? Years of believing that because I could protect our family story and could "pass" as one of the regular neighborhood kids, we would not be affected by the realities that separated us. This thinking reinforced the repeat-isms of my parents: You can't trust anyone outside the family; to be educated is the highest calling and greatest gift that no one can ever take away; nothing compares to that wartime suffering, and everything else is *over-comeable*.

Years ago, I reconnected with a childhood friend. She told me that she saw my Facebook post about Marty's having been in the Holocaust, that she sat in front of her computer and wept because of it.

"All those years, I practically lived at your house, a house that felt like home," she said, "and I never knew."

An ace at keeping secrets, I kept my family's Holocaust suffering even from my best friend. Did I remain silent to protect my father? Or to avoid standing out, to not be different? I bottled up that which should be "private" and built fences to keep people at a distance.

46

For much of my life, I resisted venturing where I didn't know if I could succeed; rules and structures made me feel fenced in.

Dad later told me he made decisions "by the seat of his pants." In my own self, I called it "intuitive and following my gut." Each of us largely avoided exposure to significant risks. Opting for safety meant limiting our visibility, vulnerability, and ability to contribute.

I was afraid to fail and fail publicly. I feared not knowing, because that meant not being in control. The result was that I often felt as if I was performing below my potential, staying safely in my comfort zone. Job promotions came when and if others recognized me, not from my own initiative. When in college, I got word that a professor was considering me as her teaching assistant. I told my roommate, "I cannot do it. I'm not ready for that much responsibility. I will turn it down." It wasn't until another psych professor got involved and encouraged me to try, that I agreed. The opportunity stretched how I saw myself and my ability to help instill learning in others (even the football team players). I was becoming more me for not knowing how well I'd do. I would have been less me for not trying.

The experience prepared me, as a liberal arts graduate, to interview for various jobs for which I had no prior experience. I was hired, learned on the job, and took on new leadership responsibilities.

47

STORYTELLER

It brings some solace that
your story will not die
with you
for your story
has been heard
by thousands of ears.
I know from stillness
in packed auditoriums
those who hear you
feel humanity rising like a great wave
I see them leaning forward
trying to understand the unimaginable.

I view time differently
now that
you and other survivors
enter twilight and beyond.
Many years have gone by

and we must keep the message alive,
for there are those who
doubt your life story
even before you are gone.

48

I remember the day I could have learned about death.

I came home from school. I was in sixth grade. My best friend and I walked in the door, and silence greeted us instead of my dog Prince's enthusiastic barking.

"Maybe he's tied up around the back," I said. We checked, but he wasn't there. "Where is the dog?" I asked Mom.

"You'll have to ask your father."

"But Dad's not here! You are! Where's the dog?"

She looked away, unresponsive. Got busy straightening spatulas in the kitchen drawer.

I stormed away. Frantically dialed Dad at The Store. "Where's Prince?"

"He's at a farm," he said.

"What? A farm? Whose farm? How long will he be there?" I was coming undone.

My friend stood by me, worry etched across her face.

Dad replied, "An electrician came to the house today, and the dog lunged for him, growling. Prince bit the man. Mom had to push the man into the bedroom and slam the door. The dog bit her. She ran into the bedroom too and called me in a panic. The two of them couldn't leave the room. The dog's bitten before, and we cannot live this way. I came home at lunch and found a new home for him. On a farm."

I collapsed in a heap and sobbed for hours. Often at first, less as time went on, I wondered aloud how our dog was faring on the farm. The story took so well that it wasn't until I recounted it to a college friend on our front steps that I realized what happened.

"You still believe the farm story," said my friend as if he doubted it.

"It's not a story. My parents told me Prince went to a farm. I don't know where. A farm so he could run loose and not hurt anyone."

We went inside, and I asked my parents what had happened.

"I didn't know you still thought that," Dad said. "The farm, it seemed kinder than telling you we had to put him down. You loved him so much. We didn't know how to tell you."

On a gut level, I must have known the truth. Dad wanted to protect me, his child, from the anguish of a grueling separation. As he did with details of his concentration camp experience, he spared me the full-on agony of loss. Offering instead the salve of kind omission and saving himself the recollection of his pain and suffering in the process. But were the two of us being spared? Or deprived of the chance to grapple with the death of loved ones and move on?

49

By the time I was ten years old, I had realized we were missing half of our relatives, and there was no trace of their ever having existed. This detail I could not, *would not*, share with anyone. I could hear others asking, "Where did they go?" And this, I knew instinctively, was a hideous thing for someone not in my family to ponder. That our relatives perished without a trace was a family secret that no one must know. Shoved into industrial ovens designed to extinguish evidence of their ever having lived, without our having a photograph, timepiece, handkerchief, broach, or letter to prove that they had.

This secret inspired a vigilance I did not know I possessed. The pressure to excel, to please, and to keep the secret was crippling. Disappointing my parents was not an option. At least, not until I became a teenager.

50

Recently, at Holocaust talks, Marty told me and his audience about his older brother, Moishe, who was big and strong. Marty looked up to Moishe. "I learned he made it through the camps," Marty said.

One day after liberation, Moishe went off with a neighbor and disappeared forever. The neighbor was a Kapo at Mauthausen (a Jewish prisoner forced to be a guard over other Jews). Moishe had threatened to expose the man's cruelty to a young woman he fancied.

"We heard the neighbor took him out to the countryside and killed him," Marty said matter-of-factly, no venom in his tone.

"I never knew that," I said. Then, "Have you ever searched for Moishe?"

"There were no records. He was killed after the war."

I was afraid to force the issue. But my mind raced. *What if you're wrong? What if Moishe lived?* I would want to know for sure, I told myself. But what if, for him, certainty came at the cost of a fruitless search as he suspected? What if it renewed his pain at the loss of a brother he idolized, resulted in Moishe being murdered twice?

51

I was at dinner with my husband and another couple, one of whom was of German descent. More specifically, his father had been a baron. He lost his fortune after the war. We knew where our fathers were during the war, but the topic was off-limits, verboten. It was something we didn't divulge.

In our conversation, I skirted around the edges of our silent rule, not to talk about The War. I came at the story slant, and told them about finding out on Facebook that my father's and other Holocaust survivor portraits were on exhibit in Vienna, Austria.

The man's wife expressed surprise. "All these years, I never knew your father went through that," she said. She teared up. I glanced at her husband for a reaction. He looked away, noodled at nothing with his fork. I did not perceive it as complicit or disinterest, but as complicated.

I apologized for my impolite dinner conversation. I had unwittingly shared our tragic past over dinner. At times it pours out so naturally, like ice water from a silver pitcher.

52

Laughter did not exist in our house, and I missed it. I searched for laughter on TV shows like *I Love Lucy* and *Soupy Sales* and appreciated a sense of humor in my friends.

My aunt once told my mother, "The war robbed me of the capacity to laugh."

Though we never discussed it, my father, too, was hard-pressed to relax enough for laughter and was the opposite of silly. On Mother's manic days, she could be silly, irreverent, and fun. One time she grabbed hold of a half-gallon of chocolate ice cream from the freezer and got Marty to chase her around our modest ranch house. He unexpectedly obliged. I remember how my brother and I reeled with delight.

I spent many of my childhood Saturdays at my friend Lauren's house. It was the kind of house where beautiful lace curtains festooned the windows and sunlight poured in, creating a setting of warmth and welcome. Further evidence of hominess was Lauren's grammy, who baked homemade oatmeal raisin cookies that we ate warm from the oven. Lauren's parents joked around with each other, and her dad didn't work on Saturdays.

One Saturday, we learned that her uncle, a prosperous town lawyer and frequent lap swimmer in their pool, had died in his sleep from an overdose of pills. It was whispered that he owed the government taxes and could have faced jail. Hard to fathom that one day he was swimming and the next, gone.

It was the first time I realized that internal suffering could be so ruthless that, for some, the only way out was to end one's life by suicide. Before that, I believed that lives could only be extinguished by others.

53

The year after college, I took a job at a fancy law firm in Washington, D.C. I saw it as a ticket out of New Jersey, and, after all the waitressing, I was glad to secure a position as a legal receptionist. My duties included answering multiple phone lines, typing legal briefs, and pouring coffee for predominantly male lawyers in expensive dark suits who gathered around a mahogany table the size of New York State.

As the first person to greet employees and clients, and the last to say goodbye, I fielded comments about my appearance and dateability "on the regular." When there wasn't foot traffic, bland walls and banal duties brought me down, so every day, I called my friend who worked as a paralegal a few blocks away. I also phoned the guy I liked who lived in California, which was a long-distance call. Some part of me knew I shouldn't be doing it, but I rationalized it was the only way to keep my sanity all the long days. The calls went on for a couple months.

Then one day, the brusque office manager took me aside, wagging paper phone bills so close that they brushed my blouse. She said, "We checked, and no lawyer has a client in the 310 area code that they call daily. It's you who's been making the calls, isn't it?"

The hiss and accusation terrified me, though I must have known a day of reckoning would come. To confess that I had charged personal calls to the firm would be shameful. Our family code was not to bring shame to ourselves or others. So, I denied it—and was let go on the spot.

Most troubling to me was that aside from little white lies, which my mother said were all right, I didn't see myself as someone who lied. Yet the proof was irrefutable. Was I the kind of person who defrauded her employer? Questions dogged me for weeks and months. I wasn't raised like that. I was flawed. Weak. My actions were dishonest. I was in my early twenties and didn't have a fixed idea about the person I wanted to be, but knew, at my core, I wasn't someone who cheated and lied.

When I first found myself without a job, I wanted someone to come and rescue me, to throw me a lifeline and reel me in. Just like I'd wished to have a mother who exposed me to museums and bookstores, invited friends for dinner, and could show me how to make my way in a man's world. I had yet to learn that I could rescue myself.

54

Growing up, I learned to regard Sunday—Marty's only day off—as a day of rest and ritual. As neighbors dressed in their Sunday best and headed to Catholic mass, Marty and I rose early to cook pancakes. I'd don my crinkly blue apron and tug a kitchen chair across the Formica floor to the stove so that I could see inside the frying pan.

"Cornmeal," he said each Sunday. "Add cornmeal to a mix; that's the secret of getting pancakes to rise properly." He showed me how to test if the pan was ready by flicking a drop of water. If it sizzled, then sputtered, it was time to pour in the pancake batter. Also, bubbles on top of the pancake signaled that it was ready to be flipped, a step he performed with a quick turn of the wrist.

While Joan and my brother were still in their beds, Marty and I bonded over cooking. He taught me how to make decisions during those precious sessions.

"Is it time to flip?" he asked. "Shall we make silver-dollar pancakes or regular-sized?"

After Sunday breakfast, Marty would load a Broadway album on his turntable, one of his two indulgences—music and books. At my mom's encouragement, he invested in a state-of-the-art Bang and Olufsen sound system. Of his own inclination, he indulged in two Broadway shows a year. He loved musicals for their clever lyrics and uplifting songs.

Melodies and theater afforded refuge from relentless responsibility. Marty kept a sizeable Broadway album collection that included soundtracks from *Kiss Me Kate*, *South Pacific*, *Carousel*, and *Gigi*. Predictable as sunset, and only on Sundays, he'd stretch out on the velveteen Anjou pear-toned couch, his eyelids closed as he surrendered. Deep slumber ensued. His snoring would join the soundtrack of blaring show tunes, and we knew better than to disturb him. Music and lyrics, pure Americana, reached every nook and cranny of our modest home. And it sounded like freedom.

Some of Marty's favorite musical tunes seeped into my soul. When I lived on my own, I played Barbra Streisand's song "Somewhere (Out There)" so many times that the cassette snapped from wear. I think I took the song as a sign of how, with enough grit and passion, I could become someone other than who I seemed destined to be. I craved to discover a somewhere out there more enlightening than the town where I was raised.

55

Dad did not get to grow in his relationships with his parents, grandparents, and half his siblings. He made his own way and rarely asked for help. He prioritized loving relationships with his children and grandchildren, and engaged easily with customers and strangers. His inherent wisdom, humility, and signature chuckle drew others in.

There's the way his eyes gleamed when they looked at me. Beaming acceptance for who I was. Expressions of pride that I was his daughter. Growing up the daughter of two deeply wounded parents, I felt their pride in me. Inexplicably, this too, was part of my normal. In college, I became more aware that not everyone grew up with parents who believed in them. I was grateful for my good fortune to be a receiver of parental non-judgment, inherent kindness, and common sense. To be a recipient of love, always love.

As long as I can remember, Dad thanked me and told me how much he appreciated that I was his daughter. As he ages, he has a realistic and raw viewpoint about the days that remain, but he's always had this. His capacity for gratitude is a deep well, full of appreciation for ordinary things, things other people often take for granted. A precious gift to be raised with, a kind of self-sustaining nourishment to be left with. It was as if I learned at his knee that life itself is to be cherished, not raw ambition or acquisitions. That life itself is sacred. It is not a given. We must make of it all we can.

When I was pregnant the first time, I felt our son's first kick at the famous L.A. deli, Nate 'n Al's, while raising a spoon of matzo ball soup to my mouth. I jumped up and ran to the other side of the booth so my husband could feel our baby move.

At that moment, it dawned on me that the tiny seed of life growing within me was a miracle of astounding proportions. My father survived, married my mother, and I was born. My husband and I would have a baby, which meant we would live another generation. Marty said his family was the best revenge for what he survived. So was mine.

We will live.

56

A t forty-nine, I was diagnosed with thyroid cancer, cancer of the throat, the epicenter of voice. Crazy close to my vocal cords, the source of vocal expression, the surgeon had to be careful not to nick them or change my voice. What a shock! All the years of relative silence, acting out of habit, and out of alignment with my truth quite literally made me ill. And this terrified me.

I was drowning in self-imposed and externally ingested perfectionism. My diagnosis: I was flawed.

Upon hearing the cancer diagnosis, my mother told me, "You would be the first person in our family to have cancer." As if I had been willing it upon myself. As if it were true. Later I realized that everything I'd done to "keep up appearances"—though I denied like hell doing so—had indeed led to disease.

In preparation for radiation treatment, I went into isolation and did the same afterward. I was literally radioactive, a danger to my husband, children, and parents. I used an artisan cowbell to call for assistance, that unmistakable ring. When I was sick, I couldn't care for anyone else. At first, I couldn't bear it. Being surrounded by love and taken care of felt like I was being smothered.

I bargained with G-d, "Please make me well." I promised to ignore my needs no longer. I would allow myself to ask questions, peer into what I'd stuffed deep inside, and express the discovery in the way I needed—no more wishing and waiting for a someday that would never come.

I discovered that I had been defaulting to rules and expectations that others had for me. Liberation was only possible once I put a spotlight on what was driving (and inhibiting) me. I began to update my beliefs to align with my desires. I allowed myself to stretch beyond the wounds my parents carried. Once I granted self-permission, I felt immense relief from perceived limits on who I was capable of being.

There was a new urgency to life, a new drive to make a mark. Life is fragile as a teacup. We are blessed to live each day. Why not choose to live it out loud?

57

CRACKING THE CODE

I fear I won't remember to ask him the questions
I most need answers to.
That he'll simply expire,
it will be too late.
That he'll take the code with him
for man's capacity for good beyond evil,
for awakening with hope.
A soul shattered
doesn't heal completely
and what if it's the wound suffered
that lifts impact beyond imagining?

It is natural to stumble into the quicksand
of parental explanation, expectation,
and make it our own.
Parents raise us with stories of how things are and will be
according to their experience
and we swallow stories whole.

Perhaps the way to examine family lore
is to pull back the curtain, not look away
peer through the pane with eyes to the sky
behold how the moon ray shines through.

58

My mother lived three weeks from the day she received the diagnosis of pancreatic cancer. She faded fast and was, in a most ethereal way, at her most compelling and beautiful in those final weeks—her skin like a Georgia peach, her breath a gentle breeze.

A couple of months before she died, and before we had a diagnosis, I packed her and the wheelchair in the car to wander the grounds of a nearby municipal garden. It was spring, after all. I wanted her to be among birds (she loved and sculpted birds) and flowering trees. We didn't yet know how long she had. I wanted us to feel the breeze in our hair; to break and share what silence remained between us. I told her I loved her. That I was grateful for her love, creativity, levity, and gut-smart sensibilities. Mom said to me in no uncertain terms, while we sat side by side on a park bench in view of turtles sunning on a log, that she didn't want Marty or me to fall apart over her when she was gone.

"You will need to go on with your lives. I want that. Promise me." Those words, her words, a parting gift.

She died a queen's death, for she left this world for the next peacefully on a May morning. Sun rays fluttered over her cooling, diminished body. She lay on a hospital bed in their apartment's dining room. The window view overlooked tops of leafy trees she hadn't seen for days.

Dad was as sad and pragmatic as I'd ever seen him. He had tended to her multiplying needs dependably, lovingly. Throughout their marriage, he could have left her a hundred times. He never did.

59

I listened to my father speak dozens of times of his experience growing up without a childhood. By the time he was thirteen, the Hungarians were proxies for Germans in Czechoslovakia; when he was fourteen, he and his family were shipped to death and hard-labor camps. Though he remained silent and stoic about his suffering throughout my childhood, my mother told me how Marty often had nightmares that punctured his sleep. Pain, in one form or another, is part of the collective human experience. Yet in my childhood, I saw Marty as only strong, independent, and practical.

It wasn't until he was sixty three years old and I heard him talk about his Holocaust experience at the USHMM that he became multi-dimensional and mortal to me. His vulnerability, his visible emotional distress, showed me, and everyone in every audience, a mirror for our own pain. I knew then if he could find an uncommon willingness to open up instead of running away, self-medicating, or denying, that ability lived inside each one of us.

INHERITANCE

My favorite thing
about you is your deep well of compassion
born of suffering
yet somehow, you
embody heart and hope,
a hero among us.

I have long wondered
do my veins throb with memories that
came before me?
For sorrow soaks like snow on naked skin.

Tears puddle
unbidden
for family unknown
their screams wail
through my being
from a time
before birth
as if
ghosts sear my sensibility
and steer my soul.

60

Marty joined a Holocaust Survivors' writing class at the museum taught by Maggie, a teacher who volunteered to help survivors express what was inside and put their experience into words. She intended to teach for a year and ended up staying for twenty.

"At first," Maggie said to me, "Marty didn't see the point of writing about the Holocaust, about the distant past. He wanted to focus on his time in America and the future. On topics like when he emigrated, and how he longed to learn English and become a modern American."

"My Holocaust past," Marty told her, "it isn't all I am. I don't dwell on it. Back then, I had hate in my heart for Germans and everyone who conspired with them. After the war, I made the decision that I didn't want my children to grow up with hate in their hearts. The people I hated then are not the generations that followed."

61

Dad gave his first-person testimony in high school and college classrooms, at teacher trainings, and at group sessions for judges, police, FBI, CIA, and Navy Seals. One event, held on the campus of St. Mary's College in Maryland, brought together a group of group of twenty university and college students of American Jewish and German non-Jewish background, including one Czech student, to explore the legacy and lessons of the Holocaust. I received an invitation from the conference organizer, a professor named Björn Krondorfer, to join Marty.

Björn wanted to break down barriers between the groups by creating a safe space to tell and learn about each other's stories. Björn was born in Germany after the war. His father was drafted at the end of the war around age sixteen (at the end of the war, the Nazis were running out of soldier-age men and started drafting boys and men over forty into the army). His father was posted outside Blechhammer, a subcamp of Auschwitz, while Marty was at a different Auschwitz subcamp. Imagine our two fathers on opposite sides of an electrified fence.

How did Björn come to teach and facilitate dialogue about the Holocaust? What role did his legacy story play in the decision? I cannot know for sure, but our need to reconcile with our families' past had brought us together.

The notion of being in the company of German students unnerved me in a way I did not expect. I had nightmares leading up to the day we traveled to campus. My fears stemmed from not knowing. Would the German students appear stern and stiff like movies I'd seen depicting Nazis? What would it be like to hear harsh-to-my-ear German spoken in the close confines of a classroom? How would I react to them? How would they react to me? Where were their grandparents during the war? Would they be receptive to Marty's testimony?

A palpable hardness lodged in my chest about an entire group, the grandchildren of Germans. As if it lay in wait, dormant, visceral fear was awakened. It lived inside my head and body. I hadn't before faced that primal fear of an actual encounter with a generalized demon. I told Dad about my nightmares and misgivings, my reluctance to attend.

"These students are not their grandparents," he assured me. "Come with me."

He and I entered the classroom on a stifling August morning. The air conditioner had given up, so windows were splayed open for air that didn't move. Beads of sweat formed on my forehead and neck.

My eyes went first to the walls. Yellowed papers with faded ink and curled-edge photos of young soldiers and battalions hung on every wall. War medals, insignias, belts, and other paraphernalia lay on rectangular tables. Could they smell my fear? Every item was an artifact attesting to where their families had been during the war. I shuddered. Which grandfathers had deemed my family and religion not worthy of life?

Each attendee had a pre-conference assignment: talk with their families and ask questions like, who was where during the war? What relics were kept, and why? For the American students, most of their grandfathers fought with the Allies. They displayed uniforms, medals, commendations, photos, and stories.

Many of the German students reported that they never had this conversation with their family or knew what artifacts were in their possession. Some parents and grandparents reluctantly agreed to talk, reveal a drawer, or show attic space that housed hidden heirlooms. Others saved more than the students ever knew. Some families refused to engage in any discussion, even going so far as to actively dissuade their adult children from attending a conference that would "stir up the past." Those students got resourceful. They asked questions, researched, even went against parental wishes to learn what happened and what their family did or did not do.

Going around the room, one by one, the German students told stories about what they discovered. Their pain was visible, as was their anger over what was said and done, and what was left unsaid and undone.

I thought, how courageous. How human.

When it was Dad's turn to speak, he did so calmly while never sugar coating the facts. He shared a story about his liberation from Mauthausen. "As Allied forces approached, the Nazis went on a rampage. They forced us to march across Austria, where I saw up close people shot for picking up a rotten potato or alfalfa on the side of the road. That's how starving we were. By this time we were callous—what's the sense to help one who fell into a hole? He'd be better off dead. When the American soldiers finally came to liberate us on May 5, 1945, we feared a trick, a hell on the other side of barbed wire fence, worse than the one we knew. Most prisoners didn't leave for days. The Americans had to convince us it was safe to leave."

Upon liberation, he, a cousin, and a friend wandered through the countryside. They came upon a truck parked on the side of a dirt road, a tub of lard and animal hides visible in the back seat.

The newly liberated prisoners were sick and starving. One of them put a fist through the truck window to retrieve the lard and hides. Oily hands, the same hands that had carried boulders of bondage to build German tunnels (to relocate wartime manufacturing underground), greedily devoured the lard.

Continuing down the country road, they approached a nearby farmhouse, tapped on the door, and asked the lady of the house if they might swap the hides for eggs and flour to make dumplings.

"The woman was alone," Marty said, "and we could have taken what we wanted. Even though at that moment we hated her, we were not spiteful. We asked for only what we needed."

In every retelling of what he saw in the woman's kindness, he cries.

Hope to a malnourished man tastes like dumplings.

I looked around the room. Tears glistened in the students' eyes. I saw flashes of recognition when Dad talked about places in a country they knew, curious expressions on their faces about a side of history never before heard.

After he finished his presentation, Marty turned to the professor and asked, "Did the students comprehend what I was trying to convey?"

The students were compassionate and curious.

One student reflected that he carried with him a sense of knowing—and not knowing—guilt and gaps in his family's story.

Students shared their struggle to define their identities, wanted a bold reckoning to come to terms with personal answers to their questions. They felt angry about what simmered beneath the surface. About how little they knew of the fullness of history. About perpetuation of secrets, silence, complicity, and denial. The students and I had more in common than I could have imagined.

Then the students wanted to hear from me.

"When did you learn what he went through as a child? What was it like to grow up as the daughter of a survivor? How does it affect your life?"

I had planned on accompanying Dad. I hadn't planned on speaking. But the students revealed intimate detail and emotion about what it was like for them—what was discussed and kept secret in their families. I took a deep breath and spoke with candor. For the first time, I went public about my experience as the daughter of a Holocaust survivor. For the first time, with my dad sitting in the room. When I was finished with my presentation, they clapped. But the immense relief of letting go was mine.

These days, Marty does not recall when we went together to campus to explore what was concealed, revealed, and changed. There was no trace of suppression.

Just a memory, erased.

62

*M*authausen. The concentration camp, located on a hill above the market town of Mauthausen, where the intelligentsia were incarcerated and worked to death. It was the main camp with nearly fifty subcamps located throughout Austria and southern Germany. Located in Austria, Melk was the subcamp where Marty went after arriving at Mauthausen from Auschwitz.

When Dad was invited to speak at Mauthausen the first time, he went alone. The second time, my husband and I accompanied him. I could not, did not, want to imagine what it would be like to stand on the same soil, grounds of evil, inhumanity, and wretched sorrow.

Dad asked the driver to take a detour up a hill. Quaint homes. Many windows faced the street. Dad said, "I remember women, so many women, looking out the windows adorned with lace curtains. They looked on as we marched right in front of their eyes."

Driving up the winding road from town, I saw rows of skulls planted in the ground like cabbages. Before I could truly process what I'd seen, we pulled up in front of a newly constructed building designed explicitly for Holocaust education. The road continued off to the left and wound past the center's walls. Dad told me that the gates to the concentration camp were around the corner at the end of the driveway.

Marty was interviewed on stage in front of journalists from Austria and other European countries. They wanted to know: Did he forgive the Germans for what they did? Marty was always clear, even when it wasn't an answer they wanted. He did not forgive those who targeted, stripped, shot, and starved people for the crime of being who they were—Jews, Romani, the feeble, and the disabled. Yet he refused to put their descendants in that league. He was asked whether he had any misgivings about the next generations of Germans. He had none. They were not responsible for the atrocities.

His generous spirit held both truths.

After a lunch of wiener schnitzel served on paper plates, the archivist chaperone assigned to my husband and me proposed a walkthrough.

"Do you want to take a tour of the camp while Marty attends sessions?" Christian, the archivist, asked.

"No," I said. I couldn't face what was on the other side of the imposing iron gate.

"You're here. You need to see it," Christian said gently. "I'll guide you through myself."

We didn't realize he meant this literally. The camp was closed to the public that day.

My husband, Maurice, and I looked at one another and nodded. His mother had been in Auschwitz, while his father worked in the underground with the righteous rescuer Raoul Wallenberg. We felt revulsion, were terrified, and faced it together.

We wove through the monuments—an oversized menorah, a tablet with a long list of names of those who perished at the site—and arrived at an imposing iron gate. It was locked, so Christian went in search of the groundskeeper, whose brown shirttails were creased and sloppy over his pants. His right hand fumbled under his shirt and reappeared with *the key*, an oversized, old-looking skeleton key that seemed made of iron. Had the same key been in the hands of Nazis? The groundskeeper looked grim, yet obedient, as he unlocked the gate.

My steps. Slow and unsure. Inside, we paused in silence. I looked up and was shocked to see a blue sky—the sun shone here. The air was crisp and still. We stood on a hill and overlooked...houses. I saw houses, and whoever lived in those houses could see those grounds.

In my mind, I'd needed to believe the camps were far away from towns and civilization. But they weren't. Villagers knew. They saw and smelled and heard and did nothing. We were shown where the officers' swimming pool once stood, where their dining hall sat while innocent prisoners starved outside.

We walked through a bunker where my father could have been. Except for upkeep, the grounds remained as they were all those years ago. Floors, walls, and bunks made of hardwood, ashen and inhospitable. A void whitewashed with the specter of suffering. I tried to picture twenty people to one minuscule hardwood shelf-bed. Hundreds to a bunker. No bathroom or heat in winter. I didn't last long inside. I felt as if I would vomit.

We moved to the underground museum. What I recalled most clearly was The Book, which seemed to stand a foot high. In fastidious handwriting, the book was filled with numbers written in blue ink. Prisoner numbers. Dates of entry, of death. Size of nose, in centimeters. All. Those. Numbers. Were people. And the keepers of the numbers were part of a system that began with lies and propaganda that convinced a segment of the population it was "normal and necessary" to select who would live and who would die. We visited the crematorium, located in a sterile room, a silent scream. Our guide talked, sharing facts, but my heart pounded. I was out the door and into the air in seconds.

Recalling Christian's kindness, even now, makes me tear up. He held sacred space for a fear-filled date with our family history; his job was to save history and tell new generations the truth about what happened in Mauthausen.

63

The way my parents let me go tells you everything. After college, when I was twenty-three, a plan to move to the West Village with my college roommate was shattered when she received and accepted a marriage proposal. My New York days ended before they started.

I lived at home with my parents in New Jersey after graduation and worked as an aide to licensed social workers in a daycare center for psychiatric patients. I was unhappy on both counts. My drive to leave home and a stress-filled job became laser-focused. When plans fell apart again, I was devastated. I needed a break to regroup and found it on a weekend visit to Washington, D.C., where I stayed with a friend's cousin.

Hours after arriving on a Friday evening, four of us sat on hard wooden chairs in a Dupont Circle pub, whose windows were splattered with urban grime. Inside, it was cozy, and our conversation covered city life, politics, and the singles scene.

I turned to people I barely knew and announced, "I'll see you in three weeks. I'm going to move here."

They peppered me with questions. "Where will you live? Where will you work? Do you know anyone here?"

I could not answer their questions. Yet, I was undaunted, unafraid. It wasn't the ale, though it flowed freely. I liked the southern city's scale and aesthetics. I liked that it was novel and unfamiliar, leaving much to be explored. I felt an urgency to leave the untenable situation I was in. Even though it was not the solution I thought it would be, it felt right, and I went with it. Even though it would not turn out as anticipated.

I returned to my parents' house and announced I would give notice at my job and move south, without knowing anything more.

We were in the family room. I waited until after the three of us had dinner. There was a fire in the fireplace. Not all the smoke was sucked up by the flue. It escaped into the room and my nose as usual; the sliding doors were cracked open a bit for circulation.

I took a stand. "It's what I want." Then I waited. For what seemed an eternity. I was as true as I'd ever been. Grounded in solid conviction. I would separate (again) to become more of who I was.

They were quite surprised. What I remember most is my father's reaction.

He said, "Sounds like it's what you want. I know you are ready for a change. Go down and try it, and since it will take time to find a job, we will support you for three months until you find your footing in a new city."

Their act of really seeing me, of trusting me to fill out "the how" of it all, of giving me their blessing while letting me go my own way has been one of life's greatest gifts.

64

BEING HUMAN

Other people's differences
ought not be our battlegrounds
our differences are what inform and stretch us the most.
We say, "never again."
Some of us mean it like our life depends on it.
What I do not understand is never again
still falls on some ears that refuse to hear
all that has happened and continues to happen in our world.
They rally around denial and magnetic personalities
who fan the flames of fear, tell them how to think.
I have the choice of being quiet
or of being human.

65

Once, I went with a friend to an astral psychic reader. The seer told me I would be a great success in life, beyond what I could imagine. It scared as much as it delighted me. At first, I puffed up from the fortune told by a stranger. *I will be known, a success.*

Within moments, my thoughts changed into, "Who am I to meet with such success when no one in my entire family has dared to step out of bounds, be visible, known for who they truly are?"

After initial delight at such a reading, I huddled and hid some more.

At some point, I came across a saying by filmmaker Robert Bresson, "Make visible what, without you, might perhaps not be seen." I wrote his words out on beautiful rice paper in a metallic silver pen, then hung it on the wall above my writing desk. The truth in his words made me shudder.

I was auditioning as a hero in my own right. Dad's voice emerged for those who were lost in the second world war when he was in his sixties. Mom was a pioneer in redefining how she would mother differently from her upbringing.

Standard fare for the second generation of survivors was to stay mired in guilt, quietude, or work. Many times, I'd get up to the batter's plate and choke. I'd want more, wish for it, talk about it…but wouldn't take a swing.

Making known what was unknown, unspoken, invisible with the help of those who would help keep me accountable, writing MY story became devotion, a sacred practice.

I had a responsibility to sound the siren when "being a bystander to one's own experience of life" was made small, was anything short of heroic. I had the responsibility to help move humanity forward in heightened awareness and compassion. To shatter the perception of what seems impossible (giving voice to the invisible) and to help replace it with the possible (making it visible), by daring to ask hard questions of ourselves and others.

66

LIVING FROM THE WOUND

Can you grasp how it is remarkable, Dad,
that you survived conditions that killed you every day, and
*   still you did not die?*
I will never know horrors of your childhood
you chose long ago to keep them locked in rooms of your
*   mind*
they would surface in night terrors I sometimes heard from
*   down the short hall*
knowing Mom was there to remind you of where you were
and that it was just a dream.
Though her words were just words, "Shhh, it is just a dream."
When everything, nearly everyone, was wrenched from you,
whether by starvation, disease, incineration
dreams died with them.
You wonder often why you were the one who lived.
Now we know the answer.
You lived to show the world it is possible to overcome
*   suffering.*

To show them what went wrong. How not to follow blindly, look away, or be complicit in cruelty.

You made it through without losing your soul. You found hope when it seemed hopeless. You express humanity from your wound for all who listen.

Epilogue

Inheritance is fraught with its inverse, absence. Marty is an institutional family memory. In my family, we all know it. When he is gone, we will have only ourselves. We, the descendants, whose instinctive reactions have included **imposing the suffering** we absorbed on our own lives…by keeping too much joy or attainment from ourselves. Some children of survivors succumb to addiction to numb the wound. Others live and work without healthy boundaries. Careful not to spend down our inheritance, which is, at its essence, **life itself**. A shadow life dwells where it is safer, less visible, and is never, ever showy. A life "transformed" is one that faces the wound of family legacy and evolves from it.

In these times, where souls are bared, and the innocence of childhood lasts a hot minute, it surprises me what else Dad kept from his daughter and son beyond the details of his story. No trace of self-pity or victimization. No evidence of death, no funerals of his siblings for my brother and me; we were deemed too young to attend. I remember, when one of Dad's brothers suffered a fatal heart attack, I asked what happens to people when they die.

"It is not the end," he said. "They go on to live another life. In the clouds."

I did not fully believe him then but seeing nothing to disprove it, I asked no further, relied upon this explanation so that I would not fear to live.

"Any sorrow can be borne if it can be made into a story or a story can be made of it," said Isak Dinesen. For Dad and me, giving pain its due—a conduit for expression — has set us free.

When I die, my children will inevitably come face to face with a lot of paper—lined and unlined, white and yellow, penned and typewritten, in notebooks and loose, on napkins and post-it notes. The prospect brings me no joy. Yet I will not part with words on paper. They are proof I am alive. My imperfect, inky attempts at coaxing thoughts into words, sentences into paragraphs, paragraphs into pages of meaning, are relentless. The child of a survivor, heroic in the capacity to hide my story for so long and the willingness, at long last, to release it.

Across the pages, I have questioned, discovered, loved, raged. Sometimes experiencing all those feelings in a single writing session. My children will not know what to save. They will be frustrated to the point of cursing my name. Here's the thing. It won't matter after I'm gone.

What will matter is I sat, and I wrote, not knowing what would become of all the words.

MARTY'S MOTHER, GOLDA, DATE AND LOCATION UNKNOWN. IT IS THE ONLY SURVIVING PORTRAIT OF HIS FAMILY OF 11 BEFORE WWII

GAIL GASPAR, AGE 2, WITH HER PARENTS AT
A COUSIN'S BAR MITZVAH IN NEWARK, NJ

GAIL, AGE 4, WITH HER BROTHER, JEFF, AGE 2,
IN FRONT OF THEIR HOME IN 1962

GAIL, AGE 6, WITH HER MOTHER, JOAN

GAIL AT HER WRITING DESK AS A COLLEGE SENIOR

Olympic Torch handoff in Washington, D.C.,
December 21, 2001 (USHMM credit)

Marty running the Olympic Torch Relay, Washington, D.C.,
December 21, 2001

FAMILY PHOTO WITH COUSINS AFTER THE OLYMPIC TORCH RELAY
ON DECEMBER 21, 2001

MARTY AND JOAN AT THE UNITED STATES HOLOCAUST
MEMORIAL SURVIVOR DINNER AROUND 2006

Marty speaking at the First Person Speaker Series
at the United States Holocaust Memorial Museum

White House Menorah Lighting Ceremony on December 5, 2013

White House Menorah Lighting Ceremony with President
and Michelle Obama on December 5, 2013

Marty presenting with Barbara Glueck, Director of the
Mauthausen Memorial, at a conference on September 22, 2014

Marty poses in front of his portrait by artist
Luigi Toscano on the National Mall in
Washington, D.C. in April 2018

Acknowledgments

Writing has nourished me for as long as I remember and in countless ways. It has taught me to pay attention to my thoughts and that a simple thing like putting pen to paper could bring sacred joy.

This book grew out of taking the leap to become a coach in midlife and the non-linear path of life and work experiences that came before. Once I uncovered the liberation of living and working in alignment with who I really was, I wanted to help other people break through their perceived limitations and experience the intrinsic joy for themselves.

Thank you to everyone who provided encouragement, support, and community as I wrote this book.

With gratitude to my wise coach, Tanya Geisler, who insisted this was the book I needed to write first. You helped me believe that telling my story and completing a book was not only doable, it was necessary.

Special thanks to my husband, Maurice, for his unwavering partnership and belief.

Thanks to Steve Kotler, the first person outside of my family who made me feel seen and encouraged me to write.

Thank you to Mendel Bluming, who showed me what faith looks like and shows up at all the right moments.

Thank you to Betsy Anthony, Yvonne Distenfeld, Kelly Rubenstein, and Stephanie Gaspar for being early readers of these pages and providing valuable feedback. Your suggestions made this a better book.

To my daughter Stephanie, I'll always love you to the moon and back. Your big heart, independent spirit and resilience make me a better person. I know you would make the women in our family who did not get the opportunity to live up to their potential very proud.

To my son Michael, thanks for your levity, encouragement, and for creating the illustrated author sketch that will forever grace this book.

To my sister-friends, Betsy Gorgei, Susan Bierman, Rochelle Ochfeld, Diane Rosen, and Sharon Weiss, and with a special shout-out to Jeff Weiss and my second generation cousins in the U.S. and Israel. Related by more than blood, they contend with their own variations of the Holocaust legacy.

To Monique Moss, whose PR skills helped get this book in front of more readers who would benefit.

To Pamela Slim and Tara Mohr, who modeled what I needed to see up close: entrepreneurial leadership, authenticity, creative self-expression, and power of women in community.

Deborah Kevin, my amazing editor, saw my book before I did and helped sculpt it into being with skill, encouragement, and generosity. Your devotion to my book helped carry me through the process.

To Joyce Moss, for our rich friendship, encouraging me to find my writer's voice and bringing a masterful editor's eye to my book.

To Martha Bullen, for being a font of wisdom, experience, and generosity about publishing my book and Christy Collins for the beautiful cover and interior design.

To my hundreds of coaching clients who inspire me alongside my guiding them.

To the authors whose words filled me with wonder and whose words and examples I took to heart, including Madeline L'Engle, Dani Shapiro, Ann Patchett, Anne Lamott, Mary Karr, Julia Cameron, and Steven Pressfield.

To all the readers of *Carrying My Father's Torch*, please believe me when I say you are never too old and it is never too late to create what matters to your heart. That I found a way to mine for meaning from my family's wound and perception of legacy limitation to write this book, means that you, too, can overcome your own fear of not knowing, and grow it into something bigger and more visible than you.

Finally, I am inspired by all those who dare greatly to understand better and overcome perceived limitations passed on to them through inheritance. I hope I have honored them with my words.

Questions for Discussion

1. What did you learn from reading the book?
2. What part of the book did you find most memorable?
3. What is a legacy belief or trauma that took root in your childhood, and how has it impacted your life?
4. What is the most memorable story passed along to you about your family legacy?
5. How does identification with your family legacy impact your behavior and expectations in life?
6. Which family member do you most identify with and why?
7. Who in your family do you admire because they are not afraid to be themselves?
8. Which family stories are a source of pride for you?
9. Are there any parts of your family's narrative that keep you from expressing your truth?
10. Which family stories or beliefs make you feel limited, stuck, or small?
11. What role have you played in keeping certain parts of the family story unspoken and hidden?
12. What are the benefits and costs of maintaining the status quo?

13. Imagine what it would be like to release the legacy limitation that holds you back and transform it into a source of strength. What would that be like? How would that change you?

ABOUT THE AUTHOR

GAIL GASPAR is a certified coach and an executive career strategist. She has a B.A. in Psychology from Ithaca College, an M.A. in Education/Human Resource Development from The George Washington University, and Professional Certifications from both The Coaches Training Institute (CTI) and International Coach Federation (ICF).

Gail's signature coaching program, Leading True, has guided hundreds of clients around the globe to move beyond perception of limitations and decision paralysis and become bolder leaders in their career and life. She has worked as a management consultant, a wellness consultant, in career development, as a strategic leader in companies and a project manager and fundraiser for non-profits.

She was Board Chair of the Bearing Witness Program, which introduced Holocaust education into U.S. Catholic schools with the Anti-Defamation League, and has been a supporter of education and development outreach for the United States Holocaust Memorial Museum.

Gail enjoys hiking, biking, running, and photography. She continues the family tradition of cooking for family and friends. Gail lives with her husband and labradoodle near Washington, D.C.

RESOURCES AT GAILGASPAR.COM

 In addition to offering leadership coaching, courses, and speaking, Gail writes a blog and newsletter which provide actionable tips and inspirational stories for those who want to be successful on their own terms without sacrificing a fulfilling life.

Please go to GailGaspar.com/Carrying-the-Torch to contact the author, place bulk orders, request a personalized inscription, and learn more about book talks and signings.

FOLLOW GAIL ON SOCIAL MEDIA

Facebook: https://www.facebook.com/GailGasparCoachAuthor/
Instagram: https://instagram.com/gail.gaspar
LinkedIn: https://www.linkedin.com/in/gailgaspar/
Twitter: https://twitter.com/coachgailg

CPSIA information can be obtained
at www.ICGtesting.com
Printed in the USA
LVHW050208281220
675097LV00013B/1516

9 781735 814209